Reflective Knowledge

Reflective Knowledge argues for a reflective virtue epistemology based on a kind of virtuous circularity found explicitly or just below the surface in the epistemological writings of Descartes, Moore, and now Davidson, who on Sosa's reading also relies crucially on an assumption of virtuous circularity. Along the way various lines of objection are explored.

In Part I Sosa considers historical alternatives to the view developed in Part II. He begins with G.E. Moore's legendary proof, and the epistemology that lies behind it. That leads to classical foundationalism, a more general position encompassing the indirect realism advocated by Moore. Next he turns to the quietist naturalism of David Hume, Ludwig Wittgenstein, and P.F. Strawson. After that comes Thomas Reid's commonsense alternative. A quite different option is the subtle and complex epistemology developed by Wilfrid Sellars over the course of a long career. Finally, Part I concludes with a study of Donald Davidson's distinctive form of epistemology naturalized (as Sosa argues).

The second part of the book presents an alternative beyond the historical positions of Part I, a virtue epistemology combined with epistemic circularity. This alternative retains elements of the earlier approaches, while discarding what was found wanting in them.

Ernest Sosa is Board of Governors Professor of Philosophy at Rutgers, the State University of New Jersey.

Reflective Knowledge

Apt Belief and Reflective Knowledge, Volume II

Ernest Sosa

CLARENDON PRESS · OXFORD

OXFORD

UNIVERSITY PRESS

Great Clarendon Street, Oxford OX2 6DP

Oxford University Press is a department of the University of Oxford.
It furthers the University's objective of excellence in research, scholarship,
and education by publishing worldwide in

Oxford New York

Auckland Cape Town Dar es Salaam Hong Kong Karachi
Kuala Lumpur Madrid Melbourne Mexico City Nairobi
New Delhi Shanghai Taipei Toronto

With offices in

Argentina Austria Brazil Chile Czech Republic France Greece
Guatemala Hungary Italy Japan Poland Portugal Singapore
South Korea Switzerland Thailand Turkey Ukraine Vietnam

Oxford is a registered trade mark of Oxford University Press
in the UK and in certain other countries

Published in the United States
by Oxford University Press Inc., New York

© Ernest Sosa 2009

The moral rights of the authors have been asserted
Database right Oxford University Press (maker)

First published 2009
First published in paperback 2011

British Library Cataloguing in Publication Data

Data available

Library of Congress Cataloging in Publication Data

Data available

Typeset by SPI Publisher Services, Pondicherry, India
Printed in Great Britain
on acid-free paper by
MPG Books Group, Bodmin and King's Lynn

ISBN 978–0–19–921725–0 (Hbk.)
ISBN 978–0–19–959636–2 (Pbk.)

10 9 8 7 6 5 4 3 2 1

Acknowledgments

At Oxford I enjoyed the social and intellectual hospitality of Gonzalo Rodriguez Pereyra, as I worked on the lectures that made up the first of these two volumes. That first volume also benefited from comments by Dennis Whitcomb. For helpful suggestions about this second volume, on both its substance and its structure, my thanks to Pavel Davydov. Thanks are due as well to friends and colleagues (in addition to those acknowledged in the first volume) for helpful discussion about these topics specifically, at one or another stage over the course of many years: Bill Alston, Guy Axtell, Paul Boghossian, Laurence BonJour, Fernando Broncano, Earl Conee, Jonathan Kvanvig, Manolo Liz, Nenad Miscevic, Ram Neta, Carlos Pereda, Al Plantinga, Duncan Pritchard, the late Eduardo Rabossi, Josh Schechter, Matthias Steup, Margarita Valdés, and Jesús Vega.

Contents

Preface

Much epistemology through the ages, right up to the most recent journal issues, is motivated by a desire to avoid circles considered vicious. How this motivation can be deeply misleading has been my topic in several widely scattered publications. This book gathers that work into one whole consisting of ten chapters. I argue for a reflective virtue epistemology based on a kind of virtuous circularity that may be found explicitly or just below the surface in the epistemological writings of Descartes, Moore, and now Davidson, who on my reading also relies crucially on an assumption of virtuous circularity. Along the way various lines of objection are explored, due respectively to Barry Stroud, William Alston, Wilfrid Sellars, and Michael Williams.

Part I considers historical alternatives to the view developed in Part II. We begin with G. E. Moore's legendary proof, and the epistemology that lies behind it. That leads to classical foundationalism, a more general position encompassing the indirect realism advocated by Moore. Next we turn to the quietist naturalism found in David Hume, Ludwig Wittgenstein, and P. F. Strawson. After that comes Thomas Reid's commonsense alternative. A quite different option is the subtle and complex epistemology developed by Wilfrid Sellars over the course of a long career. Finally, Part I concludes with a study of Donald Davidson's distinctive form of epistemology naturalized (as I argue).

The second part of the book presents an alternative beyond the historical positions of Part I, one that defends a virtue epistemology combined with epistemic circularity. This alternative retains elements of the earlier approaches, while discarding what was found wanting in them.

Some of the chapters to follow consist of previously published papers, now variously revised; others combine earlier work with the help of new connecting and supplementary material. Combined thus into a new whole, these materials may help to show how the present approach fits in an epistemological tradition spanning Descartes, Moore, and Davidson, thinkers otherwise quite diverse. A concluding chapter takes up the "problem of easy knowledge" recently posed by Stewart Cohen, one closely related to a traditional problematic of vicious circularity, the problem of the criterion. This problematic, I argue, admits a resolution that embraces virtuous circularity.

Sources

I am grateful for permission to draw from previously published work as follows.

From "Moore's Proof," in Susana Nuccetelli and Gary Seay (eds.), *Themes from G.E. Moore: New Essays in Epistemology and Ethics* (Oxford University Press, 2007), for Chapter 1.

From "Privileged Access," in Quentin Smith and Aleksandar Jokic (eds.), *Consciousness: New Philosophical Perspectives* (Oxford University Press, 2002): 273–95; for some of Chapter 2.

From "Strawson's Epistemological Naturalism," in Lewis Hahn (ed.), *The Philosophy of P.F. Strawson*, a volume in The Library of Living Philosophers (Open Court, 1998): 361–70; for Chapter 3.

From the chapter on Thomas Reid of Steven Emmanuel (ed.), *The Blackwell Guide to the Modern Philosophers: Descartes to Nietzsche* (London: Blackwell, 2000): 179–201; for Chapter 4.

From "Mythology of the Given," *History of Philosophy Quarterly* (1997): 275–86; for some of Chapter 5.

From "Knowledge, Animal and Reflective: A Reply to Michael Williams," *Proceedings of the Aristotelian Society Supplementary Volume* (2003): 113–30; for some of Chapter 5.

From "Davidson's Epistemology," in Kirk Ludwig (ed.), *Contemporary Philosophy in Focus: Donald Davidson* (Cambridge University Press, 2003): 163–83; for Chapter 6.

From "Human Knowledge, Animal and Reflective," *Philosophical Studies* (2001): 1–4; for some of Chapter 7.

From "How to Resolve the Pyrrhonian Problematic: A Lesson from Descartes," *Philosophical Studies* 85 (1997): 229–49; for some of Chapter 7.

From "Philosophical Scepticism and Epistemic Circularity," *Proceedings of the Aristotelian Society* (1994): 263–90; for Chapter 8.

From "Reflective Knowledge in the Best Circles," *Journal of Philosophy* 94 (1997): 410–30; for some of Chapter 9.

From "Reply to Stroud," in John Greco (ed.), *Ernest Sosa and His Critics* (Blackwell Publishers, 2004), pp. 315–18, for some of Chapter 9.

PART I

Chapter 1

Moore's Proof

Kant thought it a scandal that the external world had never been proved to exist.[1] Moore raised a hand, saying "Here is a hand," and raised his other hand, saying "Here is another." These being external objects, Moore concluded, there is indeed a world of external things (two at least). Written out as an argument, with a redundant hand dropped, the proof is as follows:

H-external Here is a hand.

Hands are external objects.

Therefore, there is at least one external object.

His argument, Moore adds, satisfies three conditions for being a proof. First, the premises are all different from the conclusion. Second, the conclusion follows logically from the premises. Third, the argument's purveyor knows his premises to be true. While granting that perhaps something else may be required for a legitimate proof, Moore is confident that his proof would satisfy such requirements as well. After all, how is his proof inferior to the following?

M1 Here on this page is the expression: recieve

The expression recieve is a misspelling.

Therefore, there is at least one misspelling on this page.

[1] As he says in the preface to the 2nd edn. of his *Critique of Pure Reason*.

Surely this *would* be a way of "settling" whether there is a misspelling on this page, a way of proving to someone in doubt that there is one indeed.

His "proof" would be generally rejected, Moore grants, but he traces this rejection to a requirement that the premise must itself be proved, a requirement that he finds unaccept-able. One knows plenty that one has not proved, and maybe could not prove. That is fortunate, he adds, as *he cannot prove that before him there is indeed a hand*. But on this point he is not obviously right.

Consider the following argument.

Here is a left hand.

Therefore, here is a hand.

This does satisfy Moore's three conditions for being a proof. What is more, the premise here might itself be "proved" as follows.

Here is an open left hand.

Therefore, here is a left hand.

As for *this* premise, it too is easily "proved" in keeping with Moore's three conditions. Here is a *modus ponens* proof:

$1 + 1 = 2$

$(1 + 1 = 2) \supset$ (here is an open left hand).

Therefore, here is an open left hand.

And if this counts as a proof, then any known truth is easy to prove.

Our reasoning shows, not that it is easy to produce a proof, but that Moore makes it seem too easy. Moore's requirements for being a proof must be jointly *in*sufficient, even supposing they are severally necessary. Compare someone in doubt as to whether there is a misprint on a certain page, who is offered the following "proof":

M2 The first misprint from the top of this page is a misprint on this page.

Therefore, there is a misprint on this page.

Anyone who questions whether there is any misprint on this page thereby questions whether there is a *first* misprint from the top. If the conclusion of M2 is antecedently in doubt, the premise is equally in doubt, and it begs the question to just assert it.

Analogously, it may be thought, anyone who puts in doubt whether *any* external things exist puts in doubt whether this thing here, "this hand," exists. Moore's proof H-external seems relevantly different, however, from the supposedly analogous M2. Although the premise of M2 is equally in doubt once its conclusion is in doubt, neither premise of H-external suffers that fate. Take Bishop Berkeley. In Moore's shoes, with the hand before his nose, Berkeley would still reject the conclusion of H-external without doubting the premise.[2] Moore and Berkeley might even find it obvious that they are right in saying "Here is a hand," while leaving it open whether hands are internally or externally constituted. Moore and Berkeley do of course part ways on the second premise. Moore argues for the truth of that premise, which Berkeley firmly rejects. So, Moore takes himself to have proved that there are indeed *external* objects, and to have offered his proof quite properly to his idealist opponents. Crucial to his anti-idealism is his painstaking inquiry into the very meaning of *externality*, which turns out to be a kind

---

[2] Here and in what follows I will for simplicity imagine that the mind-independence that defines externality is not just independence from "the minds of living human beings living on the earth," as Moore assumes, but independence from intelligent minds, in line with Berkeley. This abstracts from a distracting complication.

of mind-independence, so that the question whether there is an *external* world is that of whether there is a relevantly *mind-independent* objective reality.[3]

An analogy may help to show how Moore sees the matter. Suppose we are wondering whether on a certain surface there is any figure with internal angles adding up to 180 degrees. Someone then provides the following argument:

T Here on the surface (pointing) is a triangle.

Triangles have internal angles that add up to 180 degrees.

So, on this surface is a figure with internal angles adding up to 180 degrees.

We can of course buttress our second premise with a proof of its own drawn from plane geometry. As for the first premise, we know it by visual perception. But how we know the conclusion is by combining the two premises in just the way brought out by our argument T.

That, it seems to me, is how Moore thinks his argument, H-external, works against the idealist, and how it works to give us justified belief and knowledge that there is an *external* world. How he knows (*one* way we know) that there is an *external* world (the conclusion of his proof) is by combining the thing he knows by perception, that there before him is his hand, with something else that he knows by philosophical means (the reflection that takes up most of the article, for the thesis that hands, if there are any, are *external*, mind-independent entities). So his proof displays reasons based on which he can properly believe that there is an external world

---

[3] Do we really implicate *independence from the mind* in believing in hands and fires? Nor does it seem right that we must presuppose such a thing *with priority* to our ordinary singular thoughts. Recall Berkeley's claim that he, not the realist, is the champion of common sense.

(which is not to say that he might not have plenty of other reasons).

There are indeed at least two different ways in which a proof can work:

> A *persuasive* proof is a valid argument that can be used to rationally persuade one to believe its conclusion, if one has put the conclusion in doubt.

> A *display* proof is a valid argument that displays premises on which one can rationally base belief in the conclusion, without vicious circularity.

Note how these notions are both relative (to the "one" who is to be persuaded, or for whom the premises might function as proper reasons). Every persuasive proof would seem a display proof, but the converse is questionable. Consider, for example, an immediate inference from two propositions to their conjunction. This constitutes a display proof, but it is not clearly a persuasive proof. If one has put the conjunction in doubt, one is unlikely to be rationally persuaded by a simple conjoining of the premises. One is unlikely to grant both premises at the time when one doubts their conjunction. Despite this, however, the proof might be a perfectly proper display proof. That is to say, one might quite properly believe the conjunction on the rational basis provided by the two premises severally.

Moore can, and I think does, regard his proof as a good display proof, and may well even regard it as a good persuasive proof against his idealist opponents. He is certainly right that it is a display proof, and probably right if he thinks it to be a persuasive proof as well. Take someone who has not seen clearly enough what is involved in externality, who is unaware of Moore's detailed analysis of that notion in his article.[4] Anyone so benighted would seem ripe for a persuasive proof of the sort provided by Moore in that same article.

In any case, what might distinguish Moore's proof from our pseudo-proofs that clearly satisfy the three conditions offered by Moore? Can we buttress Moore's position by finding some further condition for being a cogent proof? There must surely be one, beyond the three he made explicit. Take our useless pseudo-proofs that satisfy Moore's three explicit requirements. Why are they not acceptable? Perhaps because they are so thin, so unhelpful. But how is Moore's proof any better? Well, Moore's proof may perhaps help to counter the idealist threat that he faced as a realist (along with Russell and a few others). Moore's proof may help that way, at least when combined with his inquiry into what it is to be external, and on how and why hands qualify as external, an inquiry that takes up most of his article.

In order to understand Moore's proof it is important to consider its intended target. It is normally thought to be aimed at the skeptic, but Moore's target was not so much the skeptic as the idealist. He was opposing those who think that there is no external world, that empirical reality is internal (to our minds). Against these he aimed to show that there is an *external* world, one that contains hands and other such ordinary objects.[5]

---

[4] "Proof of an External World," *Proceedings of the British Academy* 25 (1939); reprinted in *Philosophical Papers* (New York: Collier Books, 1962), pp. 126–48.

[5] True, he also opposed the view that anything we cannot prove must be accepted on faith. Of course, *this* view he did not oppose by means of his proof. He opposed it rather by remarks such as the following, addressed to those who try to cast doubt on his knowledge of the premise that there before him was his hand: "How absurd it would be to suggest that I did not know it, but only

If Moore's target is mainly the idealist, not the skeptic, this puts in question a recent interpretation of his proof as just ironic:

[On Moore's] . . . view, both the skeptic and the philosopher who tries to provide the proof demanded by the skeptic accept an unjustified theory of what knowledge consists in. This diagnosis brings out the ironic nature of Moore's presentation. Would anyone who believed that a proof of the external world was needed be satisfied by Moore's proof? No. Anyone who demanded such a proof would already have accepted the skeptic's restrictive conception of what knowledge is, and so would deny that Moore knew that he was holding up his hand. What then was Moore's purpose in presenting his proof? It was to show that there is no need for such a proof in the first place. What he wants us to see is that if there is scandal to philosophy in all of this, it is not the inability of philosophers to satisfy the demands of the skeptic; rather it is their uncritical acceptance of the legitimacy and presuppositions of their demands.[6]

Maybe Moore did want to call into question such uncritical acceptance. In fact, I am confident that he did, though we shall find below how unusual and surprising was his way of doing so. Nevertheless, he was also utterly serious in offering his proof. Given how much of his article is devoted to establishing the nature of externality and the fact that hands count as external, there can be little doubt that he was serious in his attempt to *establish* a certain conclusion: namely,

---

believed it, and that perhaps it was not the case! You might as well suggest that I do not know that I am now standing up and talking—that perhaps after all I'm not, and that it's not quite certain that I am!" ("Proof of an External World," ibid., p. 145.)

[6] This is from the chapter on Moore in Scott Soames, *Philosophical Analysis in the Twentieth Century*, vol. I (Princeton: Princeton University Press, 2003), p. 23.

that, *contra* the idealist, there is indeed an *external* world, one populated by hands among many other items.[7]

In line with that distinction between contra-skeptic and contra-idealist proofs, consider the following:

> H-general   There are hands (at least one).
>
> Hands are external objects.
>
> Therefore, there is an external world.

This, I believe, functions about as well as Moore's actual proof, H-external, against his target idealists. And it functions about as well even if one's knowledge of the first premise is at the time not at all perceptual but only a piece of standing commonsense knowledge. Even so, this *is* a proof of the external world about as good as Moore's own proof. True, the premise here *can* be proved, or so Moore would have insisted. But the fact that its first premise is provable certainly would not disqualify H-general from being a proper proof.

So, H-general can still function as a proof in the way Moore took his own proof H-external to function, in opposition to the idealist. By contrast, H-general is obviously useless against the traditional external-world skeptic. What this skeptic wants, after all, is evidence for the proposition that there are indeed such things as hands, *whether external or not*, evidence that will establish that proposition just through our use of reason and of what is given to us in experience (or in experience and immediate memory).

Moore is at pains to prove not so much that hands exist but that they are external, and thereby that there is an external world. And this he can prove against the idealist

---

[7] The idealism opposed is clearly *anthropic* idealism, which denies the existence of a world external to *human* consciousness, and not just *subjective* idealism, which denies the existence of a world external to the subject's mind.

by relying not on perception but just on his background knowledge that there are hands. Thus, he can use H-general in place of H-external. By contrast, no proof that engages the traditional external-world skeptic can start from the premise of H-general or any such general claim. One could hardly argue against the traditional skeptic about the world around us by taking it for granted as a premise that hands just do exist in the world (whatever their ontological nature). Whatever may be the right ontology of hands—whether hands are independently real, or on the contrary socially constituted—our skeptic will in any case want their existence demonstrated through reasoning from the given. What the traditional external-world skeptic puts in doubt is precisely the existence of such objects *beyond the mind of the subject.* Therefore, one cannot just assume as a premise that there are such objects. Such objects beyond the mind of the subject remain in doubt for our skeptic, moreover, regardless of whether they are external or socially mind-constituted.

Against a familiar traditional external-world skeptic, then, Moore does not and would not argue just by way of H-general, nor even by way of H-external. A direct response to that traditional skeptic requires that we reason just from our given states of consciousness enjoyed at the time or remembered from the very recent past. But wait: Does Moore perhaps reject any such requirement as that imposed by our skeptic: namely, the requirement that any real knowledge of the external world around us must be founded on the given through reason? No, actually, Moore quite clearly agrees with our skeptic on that much.[8]

---

[8] So, Moore's proof cannot have been just an ironic way of rejecting the foundationalist demands of our traditional skeptic.

How and why Moore agrees with the sort of foundation-alism presupposed by our external-world skeptic emerges in three closely related papers from a short span in the early years of the Second World War. One, "Proof of an External World,"[9] was his British Academy lecture in 1939. The other two—"Certainty"[10] and "Four Forms of Scepticism"[11] — developed as he taught and lectured in the States for the next few years.

As emerges in these papers, to give a proof is, for Moore, a performance, perhaps a public performance: one must rehearse an argument, perhaps in words. Only reasons one might proffer can possibly constitute a proof. But in his view you cannot possibly *cite* the full set of reasons that support your belief that you are awake. Here is how he puts it:

How am I to prove now that "Here's one hand and here's another"? I do not believe I can do it. In order to do it, I should need to prove for one thing, as Descartes pointed out, that I am not now dreaming. But how can I prove that I am not? I have, no doubt, conclusive reasons for asserting that I am not now dreaming; I have conclusive evidence that I am awake; but that is a very different thing from being able to prove it. I could not tell you what all my evidence is; and I should require to do this at least, in order to give you a proof.[12]

So, Moore distinguishes having reasons to believe some-thing, *even conclusive reasons*, from being able to prove it. One crucial respect of difference is that a set of reasons need not be publicly articulable, whereas a proof that can be given to others must be. Moore in fact leaves it open that a set of reasons need not even be *privately* articulable, *in foro interno*.

[9] See n. 4, above.   [10] *Philosophical Papers*, pp. 223–46.
[11] Ibid., pp. 193–222.
[12] "Proof of an External World," penultimate para.

This is why in his view one cannot prove that one is now awake: Although one's belief that one is awake is based on evidence, on conclusive reasons, *these are reasons one could not fully cite, perhaps not even to oneself*.

Moore claims that, despite his inability to prove his claim that he is holding up a hand, he still knows the truth of what he claims (since one can know things that one cannot prove). But he is *not* thereby endorsing epistemic foundationalism. He is not endorsing the doctrine that some knowledge depends not at all on evidence or reasons. Take the fact that he is then awake. According to Moore, he is unable to prove that fact, but he *does* have reasons for believing it, indeed *conclusive* reasons. To know without proof, then, is not to know without reasons. One can know based on conclusive reasons without knowing based on any proof.

Although, as it turns out, Moore is not endorsing epistemic foundationalism in "Proof of an External World," he does endorse it in another paper of the period, "Four Forms of Scepticism." There, in agreement with Russell, he has this to say:

I think I do know *immediately* things about myself . . . But I cannot help agreeing with Russell that I never know immediately such a thing as "That person is conscious" or "This is a pencil," and that also the truth of such propositions never follows logically from anything which I do know immediately, and yet I think that I do know such things for certain.[13]

Moore agrees with Russell that

(a) to know is to know for certain,[14] and, further, that

---

[13] "Four Forms of Scepticism," penultimate para.
[14] In the concluding pages of "Four Forms of Scepticism," for example, he repeatedly uses the two expressions as if they were interchangeable.

(b) our knowledge of the world around us, including neighboring minds, is derived from what we know immediately, is derived through reasoning that is not deductive but inductive or analogical.

From these premises Russell concludes that we lack knowledge of our surroundings, and must settle for probable opinion. By contrast, Moore concludes that we can enjoy knowledge for certain of our surroundings, and that such knowledge does not require deductive *proof*; it can derive rather from reasoning that is inductive or analogical.

The assumption that Moore and Russell share is not obviously true. I mean the assumption that knowledge must be knowledge for certain. At a minimum we must distinguish *absolute* certainty from a certainty that allows one to be more certain of one thing than of another. This distinction opens up a possibility: One might now cater to what is plausible in Russell's claim that non-deductive inference cannot yield certainty (absolute certainty), while agreeing with Moore that it can still deliver the level of certainty (a high enough degree of certainty) requisite for knowledge.[15]

Since our focus here is on Moore, let us adopt the sense of the word certainty compatible with his view, agreeing thus with him that one can know, and know for certain, things that one must base non-deductively (through inductive or analogical reasoning) on what one knows immediately. Having taken Moore's side on this much, we may now be baffled by the third of his three papers from those early years

---

[15] A full discussion would go into the subtle and complex ways in which knowledge, certainty, and doubt are related. I go further into the matter in "Relevant Alternatives, Contextualism Included," *Philosophical Studies* (2003): 35–65.

of the Second World War, entitled "Certainty," where we find the following passage.

I agree . . . that if I don't know now that I'm not dreaming, it follows that I don't *know* that I am standing up, even if I both actually am and think that I am. But this first part of the argument is a consideration which cuts both ways. For, if it is true, it follows that it is also true that if I *do* know that I am standing up, then I do know that I am not dreaming. I can therefore just as well argue: since I do know that I'm standing up, it follows that I do know that I'm not dreaming; as my opponent can argue: since you don't know that you're not dreaming, it follows that you don't know that you're standing up. The one argument is just as good as the other, unless my opponent can give better reasons for asserting that I don't know that I'm not dreaming, than I can give for asserting that I do know that I am standing up.[16]

But *how*, exactly, *do* we know that we are awake and not dreaming? Recall the assumption that knowledge is knowledge for certain, which we have granted, if only by allowing a threshold-dependent level of certainty requisite for knowledge.[17] And consider in this light what Moore has to say:

Now I cannot see my way to deny that it is logically possible that all the sensory experiences I am having now should be mere dream-images. And if this is logically possible, and if further the sensory experiences I am having now were the only experiences I am having, I do not see how I could possibly know for certain that I am not dreaming.[18]

[16] "Certainty," twelfth para. from the end.
[17] Note, incidentally, how, in a paper ostensibly about certainty, Moore focuses on "knowledge" (sans qualification).
[18] Ibid., third para. from the end.

Here Moore is facing the following question: Given his commitment to indirect realism, how can he account for his claimed knowledge that he is not dreaming if this does not follow from his having his sensory experiences when he makes his claim to know?

This problem Moore tries to resolve by relying not only on his present sensory experiences, but also on his memories of the immediate past. Such memories can also in his view constitute immediate knowledge. And the *combination* of his present experiences and memories is now said to be sufficient.

But what if our skeptical philosopher says: It is *not* sufficient; and offers as an argument to prove that it is not, this: It is logically possible *both* that you should be having all the sensory experiences you are having, and also that you should be remembering what you do remember, and *yet* should be dreaming. If this *is* logically possible, then I don't see how to deny that I cannot possibly know for certain that I am not dreaming.[19]

Consider now the dialectical situation. Moore agrees with the skeptic that we must be able to reason from what is given to us in experience and short-term memory to any other contingent fact that we could hope to know. Yet he thinks we cannot prove the facts that we take ourselves to know perceptually. And why is this so? Because in order to prove any such fact we would need to be able to prove that we are not dreaming at the time. And this, he claims, he cannot prove. Yet he goes on to claim about the fact that he is not dreaming that it does follow by logic from what is given to him in experience and short-term memory! Moreover, these things thus given to him constitute conclusive evidence for believing that he is awake and not dreaming. But how then

---

[19] Ibid., penultimate para.

could he have thought that we could not prove that we are awake? How could Moore have thought that it was beyond him to prove that he was awake, when, amazingly, he himself seems to provide for such a proof?! The answer to our puzzle lies in Moore's distinction between, first, a 'proof', whose possession always requires the ability to cite its premises, so that it could be given, at least to oneself *in foro interno*; and, second, conclusive reasons, which one can still have despite being unable to cite them fully. Without the ability to cite the premises one can have no proof, regardless of how high a level of certainty one might attain for believing as one does based on such conclusive evidence.

Casimir Lewy, who helped prepare for publication the collection, *Philosophical Papers*, in which Moore's paper appears, adds the following footnote about the concluding paragraphs of the paper, including the one just cited here. Lewy writes: "It should, I think, be mentioned that Moore was particularly dissatisfied with the last four paragraphs of this paper, and I believe that he was thinking primarily of these paragraphs when he wrote, in the Preface, that the paper contains bad mistakes." What might these mistakes be, and what might be said in favor of the position adopted by Moore in those passages, however mistakenly?

We have found an apparent incoherence in the position laid out by Moore in those three closely related papers. But we have seen how to defend Moore by appeal to his plausible requirement that in order to possess a proof one must be able to cite its premises, at least to oneself. Accordingly, that apparent incoherence is unlikely to be what bothered Moore about his paper.

However, something else is quite puzzling when we put those papers together. Moore rejects Russell's skepticism

despite agreeing that we know the external world *neither*
immediately *nor* by deductive reasoning from what we *do*
know immediately. In "Four Forms of Skepticism" Moore
argues against Russell that even if his beliefs about pencils,
and about the minds of others, would require an "inductive
or analogical" basis, it could still amount to knowledge
"for certain." If we can know facts without proving them
deductively, however, why not include the fact that one
is awake among those facts? Why do we need a *logical
implication* from our experiences and immediate memories
to the conclusion that we are awake and not dreaming?
Why can't it be through some sort of inductive or analogical
reasoning that we acquire our knowledge of that fact? Why
can't we have *non-deductive* knowledge of that fact?

This much Moore can rebut as follows. Since no analogical argument is likely to take us from what we know
immediately to knowledge of a hand we see, the argument
would presumably be inductive. Now, inductive arguments
come in two main varieties: enumerative, and hypothetical or
explanatory. Clearly, there is no valid enumerative induction
from our experience (exclusively) to the character of the
world around us: any such argument would require corre-
lational information as a basis for the induction. Moreover,
one side of the correlation would involve knowledge of our
surroundings, but how do we get such knowledge *in the first
place*? We seek an account of how we get it without relying
on a basis of other knowledge of the same sort.

Neither through analogical reasoning nor through enumerative induction could we know that we are awake and
not dreaming. So, we are down to some hypothetical or
explanatory induction. But note the content of the desired
conclusion: namely, that one is *not* dreaming, that one's

relevant experiences are *not* detached from externalia in the
ways characteristic of dreams. On the face of it, this lacks
the sort of content required for an explanatory induction.
An explanatory hypothesis could not be just negative as this
one is.

It might be thought that the inference could be an explanatory inference to the *presence* of a hand whose relation
to our eyes helps explain the character of our experiences.
The fact that we are not dreaming would then come along
as a byproduct of the inductive inference. And this is the
tack that Moore apparently takes in his reply to Russell. Why
does he diverge from it in this other passage of that period? Is
this perhaps why he takes himself to have blundered in those
concluding paragraphs of "Certainty"?

Perhaps; but consider how problematic his stance would
then be. He seeks to understand how he could possibly know
that he is not just dreaming, which he needs to know in
order to know about his hand. And now we are entertaining
the following way out: He knows about the hand through an
explanatory inference based on knowledge of his visual and
other experiences as of a hand before him. Once in the know
about such data, he can use this knowledge as a basis for the
belief that he is not just dreaming. Thus, he can reason against
the skeptic's challenge as follows: "Here before me is a hand,
one that is causing my experiences as of a hand before me.
But this could not be so, if I were only dreaming. Therefore,
I am not just dreaming." How plausible can it be that one
could *discover* that one is not dreaming as a byproduct of any
such inference?

Compare a case where one knows about one's current
speed only by reading one's speedometer. And suppose this
knowledge to depend entirely on an explanatory inference

from the speedometer reading to the actual speed. Could one thereby *discover*, and come to know, that one's speedometer is properly connected so as to be sensitive to one's speed? If one asked oneself whether the speedometer was properly installed and operative, one could hardly settle that matter *exclusively* by inferring one's actual speed from the speedometer reading, as an explanatory inference, so as to draw the further inference that the instrument must indeed be properly installed and operative.

Here's another way to put the point: One could hardly discover that the speed/speedometer connection is good through the following reasoning: "My speed is 40 mph, which is why my speedometer reads 40 mph. But this could not be so if the speedometer were disconnected from my actual speed. Therefore, my speedometer must not be disconnected from my actual speed."

That is why Moore does have good reason to seek some other way in which he might know that he is not dreaming. And here's how he might have reasoned: "That I am not dreaming is not something I could know through direct explanatory induction (it does not have the right content for such an inference), nor could I know it as a byproduct of such an inference. I must be able to presuppose *with independent support* that I am not dreaming, just as the speedometer reader must be able to presuppose with independent support that his instrument is properly connected and operative." That then is how Moore might have been led to require some *other* way to know that he was not dreaming, which might explain why he stretched towards some *deductive* knowledge of that fact.[20] So, this might explain why he thought we

---

[20] The problems just under the surface of Moore's proof are subtle and difficult enough that we are still struggling with them in the latest journal issues

cannot know ourselves to be awake and not dreaming unless this is implied logically by what we know immediately, by our present experiences and immediate memories. But this is really a desperate move, especially for the champion of a strong realist refutation of idealism.

None of the options considered by Moore holds much attraction to us now. What wrong turn leads to that blind alley? One mistake is to suppose that you can know about the hand only if you *know* you are not dreaming. You must *not* be dreaming, of course, but you needn't know it, not for animal knowledge. Animal knowledge of the hand requires no knowledge that it is not just a dream. So, we could just respond to the skeptic by denying what Moore is so willing to grant, as is Descartes if we believe Moore. "What is required by our perceptual knowledge of a fire we see, or a hand," we could respond, "is just that we be awake, and not that we *know* we are awake."

However, that would take us only part of the way out. For, we want a knowledge that is not just animal but also reflective. We want a knowledge that is defensible in the arena of reflection. And so we still have our problem: Although animal knowledge that we see a fire requires only that we be awake, and not that we know we are awake, *reflective* knowledge still does require knowledge that we are awake, not just dreaming.

and epistemology collections: they have figured large in the epistemology and philosophy of mind of the most recent years. So I do not suppose what I say in this brief account of the proof to provide more than a preliminary sketch of the problematic, to be supplemented in the chapters that follow. In recent discussion of these issues there are at least two particularly relevant threads. One derives from much discussed issues of content externalism and self-knowledge, and the other from the closely related "Problem of Easy Knowledge."

Although reflective knowledge requires knowledge that
we are awake, fortunately this required knowledge need not
be *prior* knowledge. Here's why.

Reflective justification is web-like, not transmissively linear. The web of belief attaches to the world through
perception and memory. But each of its nodes depends
on other nodes directly or indirectly. The web is woven
through the rational basing of beliefs on other beliefs or
experiences. There is no reason why such basing must be
asymmetrical, however, no reason that precludes *each* belief
from being based at least in part (perhaps minuscule part)
on other beliefs. *Each* might thus derive its proper epistemic
status from being based on others in a web that is attached to
the world by causation through perception or memory.

Consider now the proposition that there is an external
world. And let's allow less restrictive conceptions of externality than Moore's mind-independence conception. For
example, we might just think of the external as "that which
is to be *met with in space*," to take another Moorean notion
from his "Proof" article. It would then be quite plausible
that in order rationally to believe that here is a hand, based
on one's relevant perceptual experience, one would have
to presuppose with *independent* justification that there is an
external world, on one or another proper conception of the
external. But it would not follow, nor is it plausible, that one
must presuppose such a thing with *prior* justification.

Reflective endorsement may now take its place in the
web without any special problems. This is the key to the
Pyrrhonian problematic faced when we reflect on Moore's
Proof. That it is the key is easier said than shown, however,

and the showing is hard enough to require more doing than we have so far done.[21]

That adumbrates the alternative to be defended in Part II. But first let us consider some prominent historical alternatives. We begin with a deeper examination of the indirect realism favored by Moore, a kind of classical foundationalism.

---

[21] My own take on the problem of easy knowledge, and other problems of circularity in epistemology, will be developed in what follows, especially in Part II. Here I have offered the barest sketch of my diagnosis and prescription.

Chapter 2
Classical Foundationalism

One might be justified (or reasonable) in a certain belief because one holds it on the basis of (good) reasons. If these reasons are themselves beliefs, as they often are, then they must themselves be justified if they are to constitute an acceptable basis for further justified belief. The justification for these reasons may in turn derive from their being based on reasons of their own, of course, which reasons may again be justified based on yet further reasons, and so on and so forth.

Suppose (1) an infinite regress is ruled out.[1] And suppose (2) circular reasoning cannot fully explain anyone's epistemic justification, that the whole explanation of how belief B1 is justified could not possibly be that it is based on belief B2 as a reason, if the whole explanation of how belief B2 is justified is that it is based on belief B1 as a reason. Given 1 and 2, it follows that a justified belief must have some source of justification, mediate or immediate, that is not inferential or belief-based, not of a sort that involves a belief's being based on some other belief as a reason. At some point, sooner or later, there must be some *foundational* justification, some justification not deriving from some other belief serving as a

---

[1] But compare on this Peter D. Klein, "Human Knowledge and the Infinite Regress of Reasons," *Philosophical Perspectives* 13 (1999): 297–327. The infinite regress I here rule out is not quite the one defended by Klein, but spelling out how the two are related would take us too far afield.

rational basis. Thus are we led to epistemic *foundationalism*, and, more particularly, to its classical, givenist, internalist version.

The main problem for classical foundationalism is to explain convincingly what that further source might be. It is this flank of foundationalism that has drawn the attack on "the Myth of the Given." But the problem to be pressed here is distinct from any posed in that earlier attack, led on the side of analytic philosophy especially by Wilfrid Sellars.[2] Any anticipation of our critique is rather to be found most prominently in the writings of Roderick Chisholm,[3] ironically so, since Chisholm was himself a champion of classical foundationalism. In his view our problem could be solved without any major concession to the critics of classical foundationalism. But here we shall find otherwise.

Let us now consider in some depth the problem for classical foundationalism. A solution will emerge in due course, but one that rejects that traditional, internalist version of foundationalism, in favor of an externalist virtue-based alternative. We will then do cost/benefit analysis.

I. Must Knowledge be Grounded?

A. *Constitutive Awareness and Meta-Awareness*

Foundationalists through the ages have tried to explain how we can be justified foundationally in a belief, appealing crucially to what is "given" in one's experience, to what

---

[2] Wilfrid Sellars, "Empiricism and the Philosophy of Mind," reprinted in Sellars' *Science, Perception, and Reality* (London: Routledge and Kegan Paul, 1963).

[3] Roderick Chisholm, "The Problem of the Speckled Hen," *Mind* 51 (1942): 368–73; and cf. the section so titled of his *Theory of Knowledge*, 3rd ed. (Englewood Cliffs, NJ: Prentice Hall, Inc., 1989).

is "present" to one's consciousness. So they have appealed to objects of "direct" awareness. What sort of awareness is this? In particular, is it awareness *constitutive* of conscious experience or is it meta-awareness *about* such experience, whereby one notices it? The latter will *not* enable the desired explanation, since the concept of "noticing" is itself epistemic in a way that ill suits it for the explanatory work that it is being asked to do. What we want is an explanation in non-epistemic terms of how a non-inferential, foundational, belief can acquire epistemic status in the first place, so that holding it is not just arbitrary, so that conclusions drawn from it can inherit epistemic status. Our explanation hence cannot rest with "noticings" that are supposed to have epistemic status *already*. The question will remain as to how *these* beliefs, constitutive of the "noticings," have acquired *their* status.[4]

Thus are classical foundationalists led to mental phenomena epistemically more primitive than any "noticings"—than any judgments or occurrent beliefs—to conscious states "given in" or "present to" consciousness. In our terminology, what such foundationalists are thus led to is constitutive awareness: that is, to states constitutive of the subject's total consciousness at the time, including both states *noticed* with occurrent or episodic assent, and also ones that escape such notice. But we now face the "Problem of the Speckled Hen," which worried Roderick Chisholm since his 1942 publication in *Mind* of a paper so-titled. The problem concerns the gap between constitutive awareness and meta-awareness. Much in the intricate character of our experience can, again, escape

---

[4] Of course one can be justified in believing *that* one believes such and such, and the mere presence of this embedded occurrent belief might largely account for one's justification for self-attributing it, *even without the embedded belief being itself justified*. The present discussion in the main text abstracts from such cases.

our notice, and can even be mischaracterized, as when one takes oneself to be able to tell at a glance that an image has 10 speckles although in actual fact it has 11 rather than 10. If the classical foundationalist wishes to have a theory and not just a promissory note, he needs to tell us *which* sorts of features of our states of consciousness are the epistemically effective ones, the ones *by corresponding to which specifically* do our basic beliefs acquire epistemically foundational status. Having a visual image with 48 speckles seems not to qualify, whereas having a visual image with 3 speckles may (at least when they are large and separate enough). What is the relevant difference?[5] The full dimensions of this problem for foundationalist epistemology have yet to be properly appreciated, or so I will argue.

B. *Taking the Given*

Classical foundationalism needs foundational beliefs with arithmetical or geometrical content, since beliefs that apply mere indexical or phenomenal concepts give too thin a basis for inference, even allowing explanatory induction from the given to the external. But we still lack any adequate explanation of how we are justified through taking what is given in sheer sensory experience. More specifically, foundationalism has yet to vindicate our justified application of the thicker concepts required if we are to move adequately from the given to what lies beyond consciousness itself. For example, we still wonder how we might be justified foundationally in applying

---

[5] When he introduces the problem on p. 122 of his *Foundations of Empirical Knowledge* (London: Macmillan, 1940), Ayer acknowledges his debt to Gilbert Ryle. Ironically, the objections pressed by Ryle against the possibility of privileged access are weak, while he also spots a much more serious problem, which he fails to press.

arithmetic and geometric concepts to our experience. How might one explain such classical foundational justification? This is not just a peripheral issue for classical foundationalism. Without at least a sketch of an account, only a vacuum is left where one would expect to find the solid core of the position.

Let us distinguish among three sorts of concepts: the indexical; the phenomenal; and "simple objective concepts," such as those of arithmetic and geometry. All three can be applied to our experience. Indexical and phenomenal concepts come with a certain guarantee of reliability. The occurrent thought that *this* is *thus*, where one demonstrates, respectively, a particular headache and its particular pulsating quality, may be guaranteed to be right through its conditions of reference. As for phenomenal concepts, to grasp them is at least in part to be able to apply them correctly to one's experience. Thus, one does not so much as possess the phenomenal concept of a certain irregular shape unless one has some minimal ability to recognize that shape perceptually. This, however, is a respect in which simple objective concepts differ from phenomenal ones: no guarantee of reliability in applying them derives simply from understanding them. Simple objective concepts differ from indexical ones in that their conditions of reference fail to guarantee their correct application. However, the mere application to experience of indexical or phenomenal concepts will not provide a rich enough foundation for the empirical knowledge enjoyed by a normal human. Our problem for classical foundationalism is, more specifically, that it seems unable to account for how more contentful concepts, such as simple objective concepts, might be applied with foundational justification.

The problem derives in part from the fact that an introspective belief may correspond to one's experience while lacking justification. Thus, we need to know what further relation must hold between the belief and the experience in order for the belief to be foundationally justified. But a form of the problem remains even for a foundationalism of perceptual judgments about one's immediate surroundings. For, again, a perceptual judgment about one's immediate surroundings may lack epistemic justification despite according with one's sensory experience and deriving from it. Again, some further relation must relate the experience, the surroundings, and the belief, in order for the belief to be foundationally justified. But classical foundationalists have yet to explain adequately the nature of that further relation.

And there is a further problem.

C. A Gap in Classical Foundationalism

Despite the insights contained in classical foundationalism, it cannot be a complete account, not even of the restricted field of states that make up one's subjective point of view. A gaping deficiency in the account suggests that we must explain the authority of beliefs about one's current mental states by appeal to something other than the support of those very states.

The gap concerns our knowledge that we do *not* consciously believe such and such, and our knowledge that we do *not* consciously intend such and such, and our knowledge that we do *not* seem to see anything red or any triangle. In no such case is our knowledge based on some conscious state that rationalizes it.[6] On the contrary, it is precisely the *absence* of a relevant belief or intention or experience that makes it a

---

[6] Nor is it to be explained, as is sometimes suggested, through appeal to first-order inquiry or deliberation, as when one decides what one believes about the current state of the economy by reviewing one's evidence. This may determine what one *ought* to believe, but not necessarily what one does believe.

case of knowledge. Moreover, our belief in the *absence* of the state need not be based on any conscious state to which it is appropriately responsive.

We must distinguish between believing that not-p and not believing that p, between desiring that not-p and not desiring that p, between experiencing as if not-p and not experiencing as if p. Nevertheless, we enjoy privileged access to both sides of each such pair. The more general problem for the approach in terms of an intermediate conscious state is this: We enjoy privileged access both to what is present in our consciousness and to what is absent from it. What explains the one is unlikely to differ dramatically and fundamentally from what explains the other. So, even if the account of what is present to consciousness must invoke some relevantly distinguished conscious states that help rationalize our pertinent beliefs, something deeper must explain what is shared in common between that case of privileged access and our equally privileged access to what is absent from consciousness. This is a problem for classical foundationalism, since, again, the explanation in terms of taking the given falls short if powerless to explain our foundationally justified beliefs about what is *absent* from our consciousness at the time, and yet the explanation of that foundational justification can hardly diverge radically from the explanation of our foundational justification for beliefs about what is *present* in our consciousness.

D. *Foundational Knowledge*

We have considered a foundationalist account of how beliefs can have *foundationally* justified status through sticking to the character of the subject's own conscious experience at the time. This account is not successful, or so I have argued.

Next I would like to sketch instead a positive view that seems more promising.

What distinguishes the case of 48 speckles where one guesses right, and does not know, from the case of 3 speckles, where one does know, *foundationally* so? We need to appeal not just

(a) to the specific property of the experience, its containing however many speckles, say,

and

(b) to the propositional content of the occurrent thought as one judges the image to contain that many speckles,

and

(c) to the match between that property of the experience and that propositional content—such that the propositional content predicates that very character of the experience.

For in the case of the 48-speckled image, where one guesses right in taking the image to contain that many speckles, one does satisfy the requirement set by (a)–(c), and one's judgment does fit the character of ones' image. Yet one fails to know by acquaintance, and one fails even to be justified.

It is hard to resist the conclusion that we must appeal not only to (a)–(c), but also to the following:

(d) to some causal or counterfactual connection between the character of the experience and the propositional content of the judgment, i.e., between the experience's having that character and the judgment's having that propositional content.

This is abetted by the thought that if the judgment (with its content) is to be rationalized by the experience (with its relevant character), then the former must be appropriately responsive to the latter, in such a way that variations in the latter would have led to corresponding variations in the former. Or perhaps it will suffice for appropriate responsiveness that not easily might one have so believed without being right.

Accordingly, what seems required is that one's judgment as to the phenomenal character of one's experience be appropriately causally or counterfactually (and reliably) related to the character of the experience. If this is right, it is fascinating to find at the heart of givenist, internalist, classical foundationalism a need for the sort of relation so often used by its externalist opponents, over the course of recent decades, for their various externalist alternatives. Some have invoked straight causation of a belief by the fact that is its content, others a requirement of non-accidentality, others a counterfactual tracking requirement, and others yet a requirement of reliable generation and sustainment of the belief. These have been proposed mostly as requirements that a belief must satisfy in order to qualify as knowledge, whereas our main focus here has been on how a belief gets to be epistemically justified. But there is a close connection between the two concerns, though this has yet to be spelled out in satisfactory detail, given the unclarity and ambiguity in the relevant terminology of "epistemic justification."

I will conclude with a sketch of the sort of requirements that seem to me most promising. How then would one distinguish

(i) an *unjustified* "introspective" judgment, say that one's image has 48 speckles, when it is a true judgment, and one issued with full view of the image having that specific character,

from

(ii) a *justified* "introspective" judgment, say that one's image has 3 speckles?

The relevant distinction is that the latter judgment is competent, *intellectually virtuous*, or so I wish to suggest. It is thus competent because it derives from a way of forming beliefs that is an intellectual virtue or competence, one that in our normal situation for forming such beliefs would tend strongly enough to give us beliefs that are apt, that is to say, beliefs that get it right in a way that manifests a competence.

One does not know nor is one so much as justified foundationally in taking one's image to contain 48 speckles, even if one's image *does* in fact contain 48 speckles, so that one's belief corresponds precisely to what is then given in one's consciousness. One falls short in that case because of how easily one might have believed that one's image had 48 speckles while it had at least one more speckle or one less. But that is not so for the belief that one's image has 3 speckles.

It is not sufficient that one's belief be *safe*, that not easily might one have so believed while one's belief was false. Consider the belief that $(2^2)^2 = 16$. Not easily would anyone believe this without being right, since not possibly would anyone believe it without being right. Nevertheless, if one derives and sustains that belief only by means of a procedure which assumes that $(x^n)^n = x^{n+n}$, then one fails to know, despite one's belief's being perfectly "safe," in the sense defined. One does not get it right *through* one's exercise of any relevant competence, one's success does not *manifest* any such competence.

For that reason, whether it requires safety or not, knowledge requires the exercise of competence.

An opponent could now take a different tack, by arguing against what he alleges to be presupposed in our reasoning. Thus it might be argued first that *justification* is not just whatever remains when you subtract true belief from knowledge. Justification may be said to answer to its own requirements, and to have its own separate intuitive basis, one more closely allied to concepts of reasonableness and rationality. Thus what one is assessing in calling a belief justified is rather the worth of the mind of the believer in respect of holding that belief with the basis that it has and in the internal circumstances in which it is held. Thus the relevant focus of evaluation is rather the relevant coherence of that mind, either at that moment or over the stretch of its history relevant to the acquisition and sustainment of that belief.

Nevertheless, the basic point remains. It is not enough that one's beliefs at that time jibe in logical respects with the experiences one is then undergoing. For, the belief that one has an image with 48 speckles could hardly jibe better with that image's having exactly that many speckles, while yet the belief remains unjustified despite such impressive correspondence. What can be missing here although present where one believes one's image to have 3 speckles while that is exactly how many speckles it does have? Once again what matters must involve one's virtuous ability to discern cases of 3 speckles from those involving fewer speckles, or more, by contrast with one's *inability* to discriminate comparably as to 48 speckles.

In evaluating that proposal, recall, we seek to understand a source of *epistemic justification* (in a sense allied with rationality and reasonableness) that will be *foundational*, i.e., that will not derive wholly from any inference, implicit or explicit. It is a mistake, therefore, to oppose our proposal by arguing that someone *could* be justified in self-attributing an experience of 48 speckles despite lacking a virtuous ability to discriminate such experiences directly: by arguing, for example, that someone *could* be thus justified simply by inferring from a directly introspected inclination to so believe, along with a well justified belief that such inclinations almost always turn out correct. This *would* explain a source of epistemic justification for that belief all right, even absent any virtuous ability to discriminate such experiences directly, but that justification would be inferential, not foundational.

II. A Virtue Epistemology

A. *Externalism and Justification*

Our sketched virtue epistemology is a form of externalism, so we face a barrage of standard objections to externalism, and should prepare to modify or supplement our proposal so as to meet those objections. Consider, for example, the "new evil demon problem." The victim of Descartes' evil demon seems *not* deprived of *ordinary* justification, in some straightforward sense, since his beliefs still derive from sources that we recognize as justification-conferring: namely, sense experience, memory, et cetera. The environment changes radically, but the victim retains and uses a repertoire of intellectual virtues. True, because the environment is so radically abnormal and wrong for his normal virtues, those virtues may *not* qualify as virtuous relative to *that* environment. Nevertheless, the victims' beliefs are still justified, in some relevant sense.

It seems to many that epistemic justification is an internal matter isolated from the luck of your contingent emplacement. This is redolent of the Kantian view that moral quality derives from how it is in the subject's mind and not from contingent external features yielding causal consequences of his policies and decisions, thus determining how well these turn out in the actual world.

There is in epistemology an analogue of such Kantianism: epistemic worth should derive from qualities of the subject's mind and not from contingent external features determining (a) the causal origins of the subject's beliefs and inference patterns, and (b) how reliably truth-conducive *such* causal determination of beliefs and inference patterns is generally in our actual world. Suppose epistemic justification does indeed depend only on such internal matters independent of the subject's contingent emplacement. How, more positively and fully, should we then conceive of such justification? Some have understood it as a kind of blamelessness, as the avoidance of any wrongful violation of epistemic norms required for right belief formation. But this way of understanding epistemic justification takes us only so far, and comes up short: if you are brainwashed or brought up epistemically in a superstitious community, you may bear no blame for beliefs and inference patterns that still fall short epistemically. They fall short, moreover, in specifically internal epistemic respects, and not just in their reliable connections with their external subject matter. When you are brainwashed or brought up as a young child to believe in some superstition, and you believe accordingly, you may not be "wrongfully violating" any norms, since how you proceed is then not really "up to you," deriving as it does only from aspects of your psychology before which you are then helpless.

Internal epistemic justification hence seems *not* fully explicable through mere blamelessness.[7] How then *is* it to be
understood? It is a project for the externalist to show how,
within a broad truth-connected externalist epistemology, we
can understand such a notion of justification, or of *rational*
belief.

B. *Contextual Justification*

Three epistemic statuses of human beliefs are worth distinguishing. One is *aptness*, i.e., being a belief whose correctness
derives from faculties reliable in the context of the belief; a
second is *adroitness*, where a belief is adroit in a hypothetical
situation iff it derives in that situation from competences that
are reliable in our actual normal context, from which we
normally make the evaluation; and a third status is that of
subjective rationality, i.e., the status that a belief has when it
would survive deep reflection by the subject in the light of
her deepest epistemic standards (roughly).[8] Of course, an evil
demon victim might well be subjectively rational, and that is
an epistemically good way to be, so far forth, but someone
deeply superstitious and not fully rational might equally qualify as subjectively rational. Nor will it do to appeal simply to
being blameless, since someone deeply epistemically flawed,
internally flawed, may still be blameless. So the question is:
what further internal state could we possibly be appealing to

---

[7]   Nor is it clear that the most interesting concept of epistemic justification
can abstract from the community, restricting itself to the mind of the subject now
and in the relevant stretch of its life. This will seem implausible to the extent that
we wish to regard the subject's superstitious belief as unjustified despite no fault
or epistemic flaw in the mind or relevant life of our subject taken in isolation.

[8]   Cf. Richard Foley, *The Theory of Epistemic Rationality* (Cambridge, MA:
Harvard University Press, 1987), and *Working Without a Net* (New York and
Oxford: Oxford University Press, 1993).

in supposing the victim to be internally, rationally justified? We might say: well, in arriving at his belief and sustaining it, he *reasons* well, and he *properly takes his experience into account*, and he *remembers* well. The problem is that these all stem from states of the subject and from the causal network of such states, or from subjunctive or other modal relations of such states to the subject matter concerned, which will include the layout of the external world.

In reasoning thus, I assume that the notions of *adroitly taking one's experience into account* (and even that of reasoning *inductively* well) cannot be entirely independent of the modal relations between the contents of input states and output states, as one takes account of one's experience and as one reasons from beliefs to further beliefs.[9] Thus, *visual experience as if there is something white and round before one* is a reason for believing that there is such a thing there, but only because in the actual world such a visual experience is reliably related to there being such a thing there: that is to say, what is required is that in the actual world such a visual experience *would* in normal conditions reveal the presence of such a thing before the perceiver. Most naturally one would want the state of the perceiver describable as "visual experience as if there is something white and round before him" to be necessarily

---

[9]   A fuller treatment would distinguish between *weak* adroitness, which is tantamount to our "adroitness," as defined in the text, and *strong* adroitness, which requires not only that the belief derive from a competence that is reliable in our actual world, but also that every belief with internal or a priori subject matter constitutively involved in the exercise of the virtue or faculty be also a *safe* belief, i.e., one that not easily *would* be false in the circumstances. Moreover, a fuller treatment would need to go beyond virtuous faculties to virtuous institutions if it is to give the social its proper epistemic place, as suggested already in an earlier footnote. For reasons in favor of the stronger requirements, see my "Skepticism and the Internal/External Divide," in John Graco and Ernest Sosa (ed.), *Blackwell Guide to Epistemology* (Oxford: Blackwell Publishers, 1998).

such that it *would* normally reveal the presence of such a thing. Otherwise that same state would not be properly describable as such an experience.

Alternatively one might suppose that a certain state's intrinsic phenomenal character makes it properly characterizable as a state of experiencing that way (as a state of experiencing white-round-ishly, or the like), and this with logical independence from any modal relation that *such* a state may bear to the presence or absence of white and round items. The problem for this view will be to explain how such a state could possibly give a reason to believe that there is something white and round before one. It may be held that *it just does*. And now one will face the following prospect: the need for a boundless set of principles each with fundamental status, connecting various intrinsically characterized mental states with paired external facts of specific sorts. Even though there is no modal relation between a given intrinsic mental state and its paired external fact type, that state might nevertheless serve as a reason to believe in its paired fact. And this will be so even when, as in the demon world, that sort of intrinsic mental state may in fact—when combined with the modally stable presence of the controlling demon—be a modal *counter-indication* of its paired sort of external fact. Each such rational relation uniting the supposed mental/external pairs would be postulated as holding primitively, despite the absence of any modal relation among the mates, and even when the mental state modally counter-indicates the paired external fact (assuming the presence of the demon to be modally quite stable relative to that world).

If we are to avoid such an unpleasant prospect, it is hard to see what the alternative could be other than an appeal to mental/external pairings by modal connection in the actual world, whether or not these pairings are already determined even by the very content of the experience. If the pairing is already so determined, then of course taking experience at face value would be assured of reliability simply by the fact that it would involve believing *that such and such* based on experiencing *as if such and such*, where neither the experience nor the belief could have the content (such and such) if they did not bear an appropriately reliable causal connection to external situations where it was the case that such and such.[10]

C. *Skepticism and Circularity*

On behalf of the skeptic, it may be asked: What if the actual world is *itself* a demon world? Are we then justified? Consider this conditional:

(D) *If the actual world is a demon world, then our beliefs acquired through taking our experience at face value are justified.*

Is that a true conditional? Well, either it is an indicative, material conditional or it is a disguised subjunctive (or in any case modally strong) conditional. If it is an indicative, material conditional, then it is true vacuously, since its antecedent is false. And if it is rather a subjunctive conditional, then we are back to our earlier reasoning. Conditional D thus seems true regardless of interpretation. (Of course, *also* vacuously true is the opposing material conditional that shares D's antecedent but denies its consequent.)

It might be replied that this is question-begging against the skeptic, since it assumes that the actual world is *not* a *demon* world. But the most formidable skeptic does not take it as

[10] And something similar would seem in order with regard to inductive reasoning, though this would be an even more complex matter, with a vast literature.

a premise that the actual world *is* a demon world. Rather, he takes it as a premise that the actual world *might* be a demon world. And his premise is *not* that *for all we know* the actual world is a demon world. No, this is rather his conclusion, or close to that. His premise is only that it is possible *metaphysically* (or at least logically) that the actual world be, or have been, a demon world. And we can of course agree with *that* premise, while rejecting the skeptical conclusion nonetheless.

There is a less formidable skeptic who is answered more easily, if he needs to be answered at all. According to this skeptic, we might metaphysically be in a demon world, and we cannot just assume or presuppose that we are not, since it is part of his skepticism not just to argue that we do not know what we take ourselves to know. Rather, he means *also* actually to put in question all of our supposed knowledge of the contingent, external world around us. Mark well, he means not just to raise the question as to whether we are wrong in the likes of the following single hypothesis: *that most of our beliefs are true*. No, also put in question, along with that hypothesis, is each of our contingent beliefs, particular or general, about the external world. So it would not do for the dogmatist to just *take for granted* certain contingent conditionals. The skeptic is precisely *not* granting any of that. On the contrary, he is putting all such conditionals in question, along with every other contingent truth about the external world. So it would beg the question against him to take for granted an answer to that which is in question.

True enough, if we allow the skeptic to put all of that in question, in one fell swoop, then there is no defeating him without begging the question. Well, perhaps there is, actually, since we can still press against such a skeptic a charge of arbitrariness.[11] Why is he putting in question all propositions about the external world, and not those about the realm of the necessary or about his own states of mind? After all, it is not as though we are infallible about *everything* in these realms. It is not as though here we could never make a mistake. And even if we take ourselves to be infallible and incorrigible about certain of our beliefs at least in these realms, how would we know which of them are truly so protected against error? Would we not need to employ, in order to demonstrate our prowess, the very faculties that a skeptic does or might put in question? How then could we defeat such a skeptic without begging the question?

Nevertheless, if we are at least right about these restricted areas in which we are assured of success if careful enough, it might be replied, we can then see how we do in those areas enjoy something truly special. For we are there exempt from dependence on the luck of our emplacement, on the luck of a clear channel, or a favorable medium. With regard to these special domains, there is no such dependence on channel or medium. So our control is at a maximum, our need for luck at a minimum. No wonder the knowledge that we enjoy in such cases has been so exalted in our tradition, and has even been raised to the level of the only *true* knowledge. No wonder so many have been tempted to be "skeptical" about any other knowledge. All other knowledge would then reasonably fall below the clearly

---

[11]   A famous Reidian charge, to which Descartes also seems quite alive (ironically, as Reid's charge is made as an objection to Descartes), as suggested by the true depth of the skepticism that he takes up, which is in fact Pyrrhonian and not just "Cartesian."

show a total misunderstanding of the role they actually play in our belief-systems. The correct way with the professional skeptical doubt is not to attempt to rebut it with argument, but to point out that it is idle, unreal, a pretense; and then the rebutting arguments will appear as equally idle; the reasons produced in those arguments to justify induction or belief in the existence of body are not, and do not become, *our* reasons for these beliefs; there is no such thing as *the reasons for which we hold* these beliefs.[5]

Wittgenstein wrote:

It is so difficult to find the *beginning*. Or better: it is difficult to begin at the beginning. And not to try to go further back.[6]

This passage from Wittgenstein sums up the core of epistemological naturalism, as interpreted by Strawson: "To try to meet the sceptic's challenge, in whatever way, by whatever style of argument, is to try to go further back. If one is to begin at the beginning, one must refuse the challenge as our naturalist refuses it."[7] Strawson himself sums up in his own way:

[The] . . . point has been, not to offer a rational justification of the belief in external objects and other minds or of the practice of induction, but to represent skeptical arguments and counterarguments as equally idle—not senseless, but idle—since what we have here are original, natural, inescapable commitments which we neither choose nor could give up.[8]

II. Epistemological Naturalism

Epistemological naturalism seems a rather limited doctrine. It confronts only a limited skepticism, only a skepticism with regard to framework commitments: to the use of induction

---

[5] *Skepticism and Naturalism*, pp. 19–20. [6] *On Certainty*, para. 471.
[7] *Skepticism and Naturalism*, pp. 24–5. [8] Ibid., pp. 27–8.

and to "beliefs" that there are external bodies, other minds, a determinate past, etc. This leaves standing the most radical skepticism regarding specific beliefs about the external world, the minds of others, the past, etc. It leaves standing, for example, the skepticism posed by Descartes about the specific question whether a real fire burns before him.[9]

Is epistemological naturalism (EN) a successful response to skepticism directed against our framework propositions? What exactly is the argument from Hume and Wittgenstein endorsed subsequently by Strawson?

Again, EN draws a distinction between two sorts of beliefs: first, those based on a particular reason or experience; second, those " . . . which have a quite different character, alluded to by the figures of scaffolding, framework, background, substratum, etc." The second set of beliefs are not the products of any reasoning, no matter how implicit or subconscious. And the antiskeptical argument concerning this second group of beliefs amounts to the following:

a. The general "beliefs" that there are bodies, that there are other minds, that there has been a determinate past—none of these is one that we choose or decide to have for a reason, none is based on inference or argument or reasoning. Further, we cannot help accepting them and retaining them.

b. Therefore, skeptical arguments against such beliefs are *idle*, powerless.

c. Therefore, such skeptical arguments are *negligible*, and indeed they are to be neglected.

---

[9] The skepticism left standing concerns any belief that is not a framework commitment, which includes any retail quotidian belief with a singular proposition for content, such as the belief that one sees a fire, or a hand.

Against such "beliefs" (commitments, claims, presuppositions, convictions, prejudices, "hinge propositions") skeptical
arguments aim to show that they amount neither to knowledge nor even to *justified* beliefs. What for Strawson makes
such skeptical arguments *idle* is presumably their inability,
singly or in combination, to budge our framework beliefs.
And from this it is supposed to follow that skeptical arguments
are best ignored.

Compare now a moral skeptic who holds that it is not *wrong*
to torture people for fun, arguing that such squeamishness is
just a sign of weakness, that might is right, that the strong
should feel no compunction about imposing their will to
power, etc. How should we respond?

For most of us, there is no question of ever torturing
someone for fun. Most of us would find it impossible to
do that, to enjoy torturing just for its own sake. And the
arguments of Thrasymachus or Nietzsche are not going to
budge us (arguments, e.g., that the powerful need pay no
heed to the welfare of the herd, nor to the demands of simple
justice). Does this mean that those arguments are idle and
negligible? Of course, if the only point such an argument
could possibly have is to convince us of its conclusion, then
if they could not possibly succeed in that, it follows that it
is pointless to waste our time on them. They *are* then idle
and negligible. However, even supposing that they could not
succeed in convincing us, is there no other point that such
arguments could have?

Might such arguments prompt inquiry into what it is
that makes the wrong wrong? Might the skeptic prompt us
to wonder *why* it is wrong to torture for fun? Would it
not be natural to wonder thus in response to the skeptic's
challenge? Suppose, accordingly, that we do ask *why* it is

wrong to torture for fun: "What *makes* that wrong?" This need manifest no real doubt, surely, nor can such a question be prompted *only* by some genuine, real doubt.

Sometimes when we ask "Why would it be wrong to Ø?" we are in real doubt, and we are searching for reasons that would help us decide. That is the *practical* context in which we might ask such a question, the context of the agent deliberating. But there is also a *theoretical* context, the context of the commentator or theoretician, which requires no doubt that Ø-ing *would* be wrong. As commentator or theoretician (whether or not one is also the relevant agent) one needs no help in deciding *whether* it is wrong to Ø. Indeed the theoretical question may *presuppose* that it *is* wrong to Ø. Only then does the theoretical question arise as to *why* it is wrong, as to what *makes* it wrong.

But if the theoretician presupposes that it is wrong to Ø, then how can he respond helpfully to the moral skeptic who argues that it is *not* wrong? In proceeding as he does the theoretician would seem to be just begging the question. Is he not then agreeing with epistemological naturalism after all, and neglecting the skeptic's reasoning?

Not necessarily. Given the skeptic's arguments, the theoretician needs to explain how Ø-ing is wrong, what makes it wrong, *despite* those arguments. Many interesting issues can arise as part of that project, even when the wrongness of Ø-ing is as obvious as is that of torturing for fun. Consider:

(a) Is our claim a factual claim, one that admits of truth or falsehood? If so, are we attributing an objective property of *wrongness* to a way of acting?

(b) Is it fundamentally the pain inflicted that makes it wrong? (A surgeon inflicts pain, but does not necessarily act wrongly—nor does he necessarily torture.)

(c) Is it the fact that the torture is inflicted without regard to the interests of the victim and just for the torturer's amusement, so that the torturer uses the victim just as a means? Is it *this* that makes it wrong?

And so on. At no point in any of such reasoning need there be any doubt that it *is* wrong to torture people just for fun, nor would most of us ever entertain any such real doubt. So the point of our theoretical inquiry need not be to help us decide such an issue. Our theoretical reflection has its own objectives, its own autonomous dynamics. (Of course that is not to say that it cannot ever have any practical implications.) It is aimed at understanding to the fullest extent possible the nature and conditions of right (and wrong) action (and its varieties).

Something analogous applies to epistemology as a traditional theoretical inquiry aimed at understanding, with generality and depth, the nature, conditions, and extent of human knowledge. Here again, reflection so aimed need not arise from any real *doubt* that there is any such knowledge. Such reflection might spring only from that familiar source of theoretical inquiry: sheer curiosity. Insofar as any doubt might naturally accompany such curiosity in epistemology it would be doubt about the nature and conditions of human knowledge, and not *necessarily* doubt about its extent. (This is a crucial distinction to which we shall return.) Moreover, the same holds true when the scope of the inquiry is restricted, for example, to framework commitments about the external world, other minds, etc. (Nor is it crucial that we regard these as "knowledge," since much of the familiar epistemological problematic remains if we focus rather on justified or cognitively acceptable commitments, and what renders them acceptable, etc.)

It might be replied that epistemological naturalism does not reject epistemological reflection aimed at better understanding of the nature, conditions, and extent of human knowledge (both in general and also in various delimited domains). Epistemological naturalism recommends neglect *not* of such inquiry but only of the traditional skeptical arguments designed to cast doubt on our knowledge (in general or in the delimited domains). One *can* engage in such inquiry about some presumed knowledge sans doubt that it *is* knowledge. Unshakeable conviction that it *is* knowledge would seem to render idle any skeptic's arguments against that supposed knowledge. Is it not then a waste of time to consider such arguments? What point could there be in considering them if one's mind is obdurately made up?

The epistemological naturalist's reasoning seems to be this:

(a) Take a proposition P that we are convinced of.

(b) Suppose a skeptic advances an argument A against P.

(c) To take A seriously we would need to try to come up with a counter-argument C in favor of P.

(d) Suppose, however, that P is a proposition that we accept beyond justification, perhaps as a framework conviction; suppose we accept it as an unshakeable commitment, one, moreover, that could never authentically be based on arguments or reasons.

(e) In that case, it seems best to neglect argument A and any such skeptical argument.

Some skeptics have traditionally tried to induce *epoché*, suspension of belief re a question (whether p). Most skeptics begin with a more limited aim, however, by arguing that we cannot possibly know whether p, since we cannot possibly attain well enough justified belief on the question whether

p. In order to take seriously *such* arguments against our conviction that p (supposing that is our conviction), must we come up with counter-arguments or reasons in favor of our conviction and on the basis of which we can sustain our conviction?

Take Descartes' argument "against" our conviction as to what 3 and 2 add up to: namely, the argument that it is logically conceivable that an evil demon has it in his power to induce in us absolute and intuitive or direct conviction in whatever he wishes, even when it is quite false. Is there only one way to take that argument seriously: namely, to produce a counter-argument in favor of the proposition that $3 + 2 = 5$, one on the basis of which we might then (continue to) believe that $3 + 2 = 5$?

We need to distinguish between the proposition that $3 + 2 = 5$ and the proposition that one knows or justifiably believes that $3 + 2 = 5$. At least in the first instance, our skeptic attacks just the *latter*. Taking his argument seriously does not obviously require us to produce a counter-argument in favor of the *former*. Nor does it even require that we produce a positive counter-argument in favor of the latter. Can't we, whether we do produce or even try to produce such a counter-argument, in any case recognize the power of the skeptic's argument? Can't we be persuaded that it presents us at a minimum with a paradox? The best paradoxes are sets of propositions all of which seem most convincingly established although it is equally convincing that they cannot all be true. And if we do see the skeptic as a purveyor of paradox, then we might surely take his arguments seriously without needing to produce new arguments in favor of our favored paradox-enmeshed propositions. Instead we might take his arguments seriously by examining them for defects.

We might search for an account of just where and how the skeptical arguments go wrong.

The foregoing applies even with regard to framework propositions such as the proposition that there is a physical world of bodies in space and time. Let that be proposition W. We need to distinguish W itself from the proposition that we know that W is true and from the proposition that we "acceptably," without irrationality or cognitive fault, or, in brief, "justifiedly" believe (take for granted, commit ourselves to, etc.) that proposition W. In symbols, we need to distinguish W itself from J(W).

What the skeptic normally attacks is, in the first instance, J(W) rather than W. The skeptic adduces arguments designed to demonstrate that Not-J(W). It is therefore implausible to suppose that we can take the skeptic's arguments seriously only by producing counter-arguments in favor of W. At most, it might be plausible to suggest that we would need arguments in favor of J(W). But even this is doubtful. Surely we can take the skeptic seriously if we try to find fault with his argument, if we try to refute him. And refuting an argument *against* J(W), by finding fault with its premises or with its mode of inference, does not necessarily amount to producing a positive argument *in favor* of J(W), much less one on the basis of which we might (continue to) believe J(W).

Ironically, Strawson himself *does* appear to take the skeptic's arguments against J(W) quite seriously, seriously enough to actually produce the following positive argument in favor of J(W).

P1.   Our commitment to W is original, natural, non-optional, not based on reasons.

P2.   Arguments against such commitments are necessarily futile and therefore idle and negligible.

P3.   Arguments in favor of such commitments are equally idle and negligible.

P4.   Such commitments are hence acceptable in the absence of reasons or arguments.

P5.   Our commitment to W is acceptable in the absence of reasons, and need not be defended by reasons that might counter the attacks of skeptics.

This seems to be an argument—however conclusive or compelling—in favor of J(W). But it is J(W), surely, that the skeptic attacks in the first instance. And EN does respond with a counter-argument in favor of J(W) after all (whether this is counted as, indirectly, an argument in favor of W itself, or not).

In any case, the argument of EN in favor of J(W), and in favor of the acceptability of framework commitments, is weak. Whether we cannot help believing a given proposition is one thing; whether it is epistemically acceptable for us to believe it is quite another. Many are the mechanisms of belief inducement that might produce unshakeable convictions in a true believer, with no semblance of epistemic justification. This is especially serious for the social naturalism of Wittgenstein, which includes, among framework commitments, socially induced commitments that give form to an epistemic practice. In any case, the fact that some conviction is socially induced beyond budging by rational means is no sufficient epistemic recommendation.

III. Framework Convictions and Individual Beliefs

If EN is weak with regard to framework convictions shared by an epistemic community, it is weaker still when applied to the idiosyncratic beliefs in an individual belief system. Here EN has been defended in two ways: by attack on its main alternative—empiricist foundationalism—and by defence of EN more positively, though very briefly, perhaps from a Wittgensteinian perspective.

Empiricist foundationalism holds that individual contingent beliefs are acceptable or justified only if they have the support of reasoning or observation. Such foundationalism can be challenged to produce the observational foundations from which we reason our way to beliefs such as that 'lapin' is the French for 'rabbit', or that Napoleon was defeated at Waterloo. Such beliefs would seem justified in the absence of any observations, present or recalled, from which one might build a deductive or inductive argument that would justify them. These beliefs may also be claimed plausibly to be of a sort known too well to be based on arguments.

Strawson draws a doctrine of epistemological naturalism from Hume and Wittgenstein as the best defense against the skeptic's attack. Once the special case of local and idiosyncratic propositions is recognized, here's what we are told about them:

[Wittgenstein] . . . is not concerned only with the common framework of human belief-systems at large. He is also concerned to indicate what a realist picture of *individual* belief-systems is like; and in such a picture room must be found for, as it were, local and idiosyncratic propositions (like "My name is Ludwig Wittgenstein.") as elements in someone's belief-system which are, for him, neither grounded nor up for question.[10]

That passage stops short of explicitly suggesting that EN would defend such idiosyncratic beliefs also by appeal to

---

[10] *Skepticism and Naturalism*, pp. 25–6.

the idleness of counter-arguments, etc. If that is *not* how EN would defend such beliefs, however, then EN would remain a very limited epistemology with application only to some few general commitments. But, if that *is* how EN would defend such beliefs, then EN becomes even more implausible. The mere fact that some retail belief cannot be budged by reasons might indicate only that it is pathological and not necessarily that it is acceptable and justified in the absence of argument.[11]

IV. Practical Quietism versus Theoretical Activism

Epistemological naturalism might be defined as a kind of cognitive quietism that scorns activist attempts to justify our ordinary beliefs philosophically. Such practical quietism is compatible, however, with the theoretical activism of an epistemology aimed at explaining what gives our beliefs the cognitive status required to constitute knowledge. Even after meeting all proper plain challenges to a belief of one's own, one might still properly wonder what (if anything) might render it a cognitively apt, or justified, belief. This question might well remain. Attempting to answer it need *not* constitute a reversal of one's opinion that all proper plain challenges had already been met, *either* because such challenges had been issued and appropriately met, *or* because in the circumstances there *are* no such proper challenges. After all, this new challenge is not just a plain one, is not just one that arises in the normal course of events at the level of ordinary practical or intellectual life. The challenge now

---

[11] Compare the discussion of blameless beliefs above.

is rather distinctively philosophical. Of course, meeting this new challenge will presumably, in its own way, also enhance the epistemic quality of our target belief, but it will do so in a special mode proper to the philosophical reflection of the study or the seminar room, one that it is hardly for us to scorn.

Chapter 4
Reid's Common Sense

Can we find in the writings of Thomas Reid a commonsense alternative to virtuous circularity? I will argue that Reid eventually must face a problem of vicious circularity like the one he deems fatal to Descartes, one that, ironically, we can best escape by following Descartes' lead.

I. Contingent First Principles

Knowledge of one's own mind, of the external world, and of other minds; knowledge gained inductively, or conveyed through memory, or through testimony—all such knowledge rests for Thomas Reid on his "first principles," including his "First Principles of Contingent Truths":[1]

1. That if one is conscious that p, then it is true that p.
3. That if one distinctly remembers that p, then it is true that p.
5. That if one distinctly perceives by one's senses that p, then it is true that p.

---

[1] *Essays on the Intellectual Powers of Man* (EIP), Essay VI, Chapter V, pp. 614–43 (further references will be given in the text). Such principles are thought by Reid to be irresistibly believed from an early age, some even from birth, or at least to be such that belief in them is triggered very early, absent any reasoning properly so-called, and certainly absent any conscious reasoning, whether deductive or inductive.

9. That certain features of the countenance, sounds of the voice, and gestures of the body, indicate certain thoughts and dispositions of the mind.

10. That there is a certain regard due to the human testimony in matters of fact.

12. That, in the phenomena of nature, what is to be, will probably be like to what has been in similar circumstances.

These are numbered here by their place in Reid's list, with the first changed from a principle about what exists to one about what is true, and aligned thus with the others. Lest we trivialize the first three principles, we must not give their antecedents a "success" reading; on the contrary, 'conscious' is there elliptical for 'ostensibly conscious', 'remembers' for 'ostensibly remembers', and 'perceives' for 'ostensibly perceives'. Finally, for Reid the scope of 'ostensibly conscious' is restricted to one's own ostensibly present mental states, the faculty involved being that of *introspective* consciousness ("reflection," he would say).

A philosopher of Common Sense, Reid has this to say about sense: that in "common language sense always implies judgment. A man of sense is a man of judgment. Good sense is good judgment. Nonsense is what is evidently contrary to right judgment. Common sense is that degree of judgment which is common to men with whom we can converse and transact business" (EIP 6.2; p. 557). Otherwise put, "sense, in its most common, and therefore its most proper meaning, signifies *judgment*, though philosophers often use it in another meaning. From this it is natural to think, that common sense should mean common judgment; and so it really does" (EIP 6.2; p. 560).

What exactly does Reid mean by common sense? Does he mean a shared faculty or a shared set of believed propositions? Although the answer is "mostly the latter," Reid does occasionally mean faculties, rather than beliefs, as the relevant items commonly shared. This ambiguity is most apparent where Reid takes up the reliability of our belief-forming faculties. He speaks there of "principles of common sense," a faculty itself sometimes qualifying as a "principle" though in other passages the relevant "principle" seems rather a proposition about that faculty, one generally taken for granted: that it is a reliable faculty. Yet elsewhere other "principles of common sense" say nothing of any faculty or its reliability. Putting this exegetical issue aside, we concentrate for now on principles as propositions, including those concerning faculty reliability listed above as "first principles." We shall return to faculties in due course.

Although on the present interpretation principles such as Reid's fifth (and others) escape triviality, they still succumb to falsity. What we ostensibly perceive fails to correspond without exception to external reality. Fortunately we need claim, not infallibility, but only high enough probability, allowing principle 5 to take a less assertive form: "That if one distinctly perceives by one's senses that p, then *most probably* it is true that p."

Two other problems for Reid's proposed list of Principles are not so easily dispatched:

Problem 1. Such principles as stated seem abstract enough to escape the notice of most people. It seems absurd to suppose that ordinarily they are so much as considered, much less irresistibly and immediately believed from the dawn of our intelligence.

Problem 2.   In any case it is hard to see how we could justify belief in them without vicious circularity: we surely need to exercise our memory, perception, and reason in constructing the supportive arguments required for such justification. How could we arrive at the conclusion that memory, perception, and reason are reliable faculties through any such reasoning without viciously presupposing the reliability of our faculties in that very reasoning?

The following hopes to illuminate both Reid's epistemology and also the issues themselves.

II. Beliefs and Implicit Commitments

Adherence to a principle can be explicit and theoretical or implicit and practical: either through conscious acceptance or through subconscious commitment. In either case one is required to believe instances of the consequent when aware of instances of the antecedent, and to do so in virtue of some psychological state of one's own. For example, it will not suffice that some external agency make one believe instances of the consequent upon one's becoming aware of instances of the antecedent, an agency that acts haphazardly, instance by separate instance, only *its* agency enabling our continued conformity to the principle. This would not show one's own implicit and practical commitment to the principle: mere conformity owed to such external agency does not manifest true commitment, not even implicit commitment.

Prejudice is betrayed not just through conscious belief that members of a certain group are inferior, but also through one's systematic and deliberate treatment as inferior of those known to one as members of that group, this even despite one's protestations to the contrary. Through one's treatment of such people one may manifest one's "belief" that they are inferior, even if, when asked directly and explicitly, one sincerely and vigorously denies that they are. Actions speak louder than words.

Whether the operative psychological state is called "belief" is not so important. The crucial question is whether such states are operative in one's psychology, whatever they may be called, whether states of "belief" or of "commitment" or "adherence" to principles. The point is that such states can powerfully affect one's cognitive dynamics, what one comes to believe in various circumstances given what else one already believes, what one gives up, and so on; and also one's psychological dynamics more broadly: what desires one acquires or relinquishes, and so on.

Some such commitments are habits, as Hume emphasized, but others seem innate, as they did to Reid. Learning can surely change our cognitive habits or commitments, however, as when diminishing acuity leads one to narrow the scope within which to trust one's senses, accepting their deliverances at face value. Such revision may be principled, through principles themselves evaluable epistemically as are beliefs.

The knowledge of normal, adult humans is thus meta-perspectival to some degree. The knowledge of lower animals or infants, and even some mature human knowledge, is graced with little reflection. (Still it is interesting to explore what is required for such unreflective knowledge, especially if it may be seen to underlie even our most reflective knowledge.) In any case, adult humans do have a rich epistemic perspective, even if its contained commitments remain implicit, mostly beyond our capacity to articulate. When explicit, moreover, such commitments tend to rise only to a Moorean commonsense level, below the sophistication of any Cartesian epistemology supernaturalized, or any Quinean epistemology naturalized.

Exceeding our capacity to verbalize is not distinctive of our epistemic perspective, anyhow, since much of our non-trivial knowledge, even at the animal level, far outstrips our vocabulary. How friends look, how dishes taste, etc.—this barely scratches the surface of the mute knowledge manifest in behavior systematically dependent on relevant input cues. We know the look of our friend, which guides our greeting behavior; we know the typical heft of a billiard ball, that of a tennis ball, and that of a ping-pong ball, even when unable to estimate that heft in pounds or ounces, perhaps unable even to "imagine" such specific degrees of heft with any assurance. Nevertheless, the experienced heft will reveal whether it feels right, whether it is that proper to such an object, which enables us to behave accordingly.

While unable to articulate a certain mode of belief acquisition or sustenance, we may yet grasp it well enough to enable appropriate responses as it starts to fail us through diminished powers or environmental change. Corrective responses may hence be driven by deeper-yet "beliefs" about how to respond. Just as inarticulable knowledge of a face can help guide our conduct, so inarticulate and even inarticulable knowledge can guide belief management. What is more, and moving up a level, such knowledge of how to acquire and sustain beliefs might guide corrective responses when faculties begin to falter.

The main points above concerning our meta-perspective would remain, anyhow, even if we denied the title of 'belief' to the more purely habit-like "commitments" in our framework of attitudes, including those constitutive of our epistemic meta-perspective. These commitments would still be psychological states with "content." A commitment that carried one from belief that Fa to belief that Ga might be ascribed the subjunctive-conditional content that (Fa—> Ga), for example, or perhaps the content: F's tend to be G's—each such commitment comprising, or at least yielding, the disposition to affirm Ga when one believed Fa (both commitments perhaps coexisting in one's mind at the relevant time, hierarchically ordered). Assigning it that content would seem appropriate since our assessment of such a commitment would depend on whether the corresponding content was true. Thus a habit of moving from the belief that a picked-out item is F to a belief that it is G might be criticized if items thus picked out (in the relevant circumstances) are *not* such that they tend to be G.

That is one sort of normativity to which such commitments are subject (as are beliefs). But normativity is also involved in further evaluation of how epistemically worthy it is to host that habit. Two dimensions are here relevant: one of aptness, and one of justification or rationality. Habits are inapt if acquired or sustained in ways unconnected with the truth of the beliefs they instill. Habits are unreasonable or irrational, moreover, when acquired or sustained arbitrarily or superstitiously. So, here again, dimensions of assessment are shared by ordinary beliefs and by such habits or other implicit commitments.

The point is this: much if not the whole of our epistemic structure of true, apt, justified "belief" that is non-accidentally true, unGettiered, etc., is applicable to these further psychological states—to these implicit commitments, including the innate—just as they are to the most explicit and central beliefs. Some implicit commitments are not verbalizable, nor, perhaps, are they even conscious, and they may even lie beyond our imagistic capacities. But, as we have seen, this also applies to ordinary belief.

Our epistemological curiosity and categories seem therefore applicable to the underlying commitments anyway—and that is now our main point. We cannot depend just on habits that happen to be reliable no matter how they got there or stay in place. Once this is clear, it seems a harmless verbal simplification to view such commitments as "beliefs" of a sort, especially given how similar they are to ordinary beliefs that subconsciously guide our conduct.

Reid seems often to be simplifying thus when he speaks of our "believing" his commonsense first principles.

However, a subject's cognitive structure, including his epistemic perspective, might be mixed, with elements that vary variously. In particular, he might hold both (a) fully articulable scientific or theological beliefs, as well as (b) implicit, inarticulable ones. What is important is that his relevant states be evaluable epistemically in the usual ways, which includes both a dimension of aptness and one of justification or rationality. What is distinctive of the meta-perspectival component of any such cognitive structure is that its elements are about or "about" the body of beliefs upon which, at least in part, the perspective takes a "view."

No essential disagreement would now divide us (or Reid) from anyone willing to postulate such implicit commitments, and to assess them through epistemic categories and standards identical or analogous to those used in assessing beliefs.

A general proposition might be accepted subconsciously even while denied consciously, as when someone is clearly

prejudiced, his sincere protestations to the contrary notwith-
standing. Does the subject then believe, all things considered,
or not? Better just to distinguish the states, allowing conscious
explicit affirmation—or even *conscious belief*—to coexist with
subconscious, implicit *dis*belief, detrimental as this may be to
the unity of that mind. Do you really know that the members
of the target race are your equals and not inferior, given
your sincere, well-founded, conscious profession to that effect? Even if you are granted some grade of knowledge on
that account, it will be knowledge at best degraded by your
implicit and action-guiding "belief" to the contrary.

Whether the implicit states are called "beliefs" or not, they
are in any case states of implicit adherence to "principles,"
or "commitments" that one holds. And some are presumably
held *on the inferential basis* of others. Thus one may hold the
implicit belief, about someone one perceives to be a member
of the target race, that he in particular is inferior, based on
a more general implicit prejudice that members of that race
generally are inferior. So the epistemic status of some implicit
commitments will depend on the epistemic status of other
commitments whence they are validly derived.

Accordingly, we might inquire into the epistemic structure
of our psychological states, including not only consciously explicit beliefs, but also subconsciously implicit commitments,
and even sensory experiences.[2] And here looms the Pyrrhonian problematic, with its three familiar options: foundations,
circle, and regress.

---

[2] Sensory experiences may plausibly be assigned content even when they do
not give rise to belief, as when it looks to one as if the oar in the water is bent. The
visual experience is here correctly characterizable in terms of such propositional
content, even when one has little temptation actually to believe, consciously or
subconsciously, that the oar before one is really bent.

Suppose we opt for foundations. Can the foundations be exhausted by the taking of the given? What is thus taken would now include both necessary truths known by a priori intuition and contingent truths known through introspection of one's salient current states of consciousness, along with *cogito*-like propositions (*cogito* itself, for example, and also *sum*). How now can we know our various cognitive faculties to be as reliable as we ordinarily take them to be?

It might be thought we could do so by appeal to the foundational inputs delivered by these very faculties. Consider the intuitive, perceptual, introspective, and memorial inputs that they deliver. These might now enable a picture of our own nature, of the world around us, and of how the two are systematically related, on which we could base our trust in the reliability of the very faculties that deliver those inputs.

However, in accepting those deliverances of our faculties we already rely on a commitment that those very faculties are indeed reliable. Arbitrarily accepted inputs will yield no adequate input knowledge to underwrite the relevant picture. Faculties of perception in particular involve commitment to accept inputs of certain general sorts. Consider such a faculty or subfaculty: e.g., vision, or color vision, etc., beyond just perception in general. By entailing the delivery of certain sorts of beliefs in certain correlated general conditions, it may hence bundle built-in implicit commitments to accept certain beliefs based on awareness of certain circumstances.[3]

---

[3] This can even be applied to Reid's faculty of introspection or reflection, whose deliverances would be states of being ostensibly conscious or aware that one is in such and such a mental state. But it is unclear to what extent it may apply to the case of memory. Reid unfortunately does not distinguish personal, experiential memory (which can be viewed as analogous to external perception) from retentive memory (which cannot be so viewed, in important respects). Reid fails to recognize important differences between these cognitive subfaculties. Thus

That causes a problem for the foundationalism that would have us derive a belief in the reliability of a faculty, such as perception, from the deliverances of that faculty (among others). After all, a commitment to the reliability of such deliverances is already required for the proper operation of the faculty. So the commitment must be there already and cannot without vicious circularity be supposed to obtain its epistemic status from any such inductive inference. Therefore, a question remains as to how such commitments could gain their required status. Absent such status, surely, the deliverances of the correlated "faculty" would be worth little, and could not provide inputs inductively yielding conclusions with derived epistemic worth.

There seems no alternative to granting foundational status to some such general commitments built into one's possession of a cognitive faculty. So these, some at least, must attain their epistemic worth independently of being inferred inductively. And it is here that evolution, or Divine Providence, may have its place.

We turn accordingly to *Problem 2*: How can belief in the Principles be justified without vicious circularity?

III. How Are the Principles Justified?

Perhaps each principle is a normative principle of evidence in its own right, a fundamental principle specifying conditions within which a belief would be justified, and from which it

---

while perceptual belief can be viewed as derived from perceptual experience with corresponding content (from "it looks as if here's something white and round," as experiential premise, to "here's something white and round," as belief conclusion), there is nothing like this in retentive memory, which simply preserves a belief across time.

would derive justification. But then the relevant principles would have to be a multitude with no apparent unity.[4] As Reid interpretation the proposal is also questionable, since it would detach the principles as principles of evidence from two of the features that Reid seems most intent on attributing to them: namely, *first* that they reflect or constitute our believing as we do (indeed innately and irresistibly, all of us who are relevantly sound), and *second* that they are true or approximately true principles, according to which if we believe in certain ways in certain circumstances we will be right, we will believe *with truth*.

Granted, if we interpret the principles as normative principles of evidence, we may avoid vicious circularity in deriving them from beliefs acquired by *falling under* those very principles. Moreover, in places Reid does seem to think that the evidential sources specified by these principles do yield normative status (justification or the like) for the resultant beliefs. Nevertheless, these advantages must be weighed against drawbacks already noted. Moreover, might not some alternative account provide both a more plausible reading of Reid and a better epistemology in its own right? Such an account would give a way to arrive at justified belief in the principles without circularity and without detaching them from the attachments insisted upon by Reid: to truth, at least approximate truth, and to irresistible "belief."[5] And of

---

[4] Reid is aware of this sort of issue: "I confess that, although I have, as I think, a distinct notion of the different kinds of evidence . . . yet I am not able to find any common nature to which they may all be reduced" (EIP 2.20; p. 291).

[5] As the case of the bent oar exemplifies, what is irresistibly "believed" is not the consequent instance of our belief-managing underlying commitment, but rather the underlying commitment itself, probabilistic and implicit as it remains: the "belief," namely, that is *constituted* by our irresistible disposition to judge that a thing is bent (at least upon consideration), when in normal circumstances

course it would also need to be compatible with the passages according to which the sources cited by the principles do yield (or help yield) epistemic justification for the beliefs that derive from them.

An important concept of justification involves evaluation of the subject as someone separable from her current environment. Of course agents and subjects are not *exclusively* assessable as justified or not. Actions and beliefs are, too, and more fundamentally so. One is assessable as justified *in acting or believing a certain way*. Nevertheless, the evaluation of particular acts might imply an indirect evaluation of the agent or subject herself. A tennis shot may count as accurate or not, which will imply only a minimal comment on the shotmaker. That same shot may also be assessed as skillful or not, however, which does substantially involve some evaluation of the agent, however indirect.

Abstracting from the circumstances, anyhow, at least insofar as the agent does not bear responsibility for them, some evaluations of belief focus on the believer herself, on her relevant constitution and her rational procedure. Such evaluations take into account only factors internal to the mind of the subject, not only beliefs but also experiences. Evaluations of a belief as justified or not hence take into account proceedings downstream from experience. Only if such proceedings manifest cognitive virtue are the outcome beliefs justified. And how do we assess whether a procedure does or does not manifest virtue so as to make its output belief justified, and even a case of knowledge? No alternative seems more plausible for the determination of *epistemic* or *cognitive* virtue than

we are presented with a certain appearance of something bent. The probabilistic character of the content reflects the fact that we do allow exceptions, as with the bent oar.

that of truth-conduciveness. *Understanding* will matter too, however: knowing the whys and wherefores, especially on important issues pregnant with explanatory (and predictive) payoff. And such understanding is intimately connected with coherence, since the explanatory interrelationship among our beliefs is bound to function as a, or even *the* main component of epistemically efficacious coherence.

IV. Commitment to Principles as Inference Patterns. How Are These Justified?

Jungle guides, farming peasants, and experienced sailors embody practical lore that they cannot articulate. A certain gestalt look of the environment will prompt practically appropriate inferences: that a storm is coming, say, even if the knowledge embodied must remain inarticulate: the knowledge that when the sea and the heavens look a certain way, a storm is likely brewing. Acceptance of the fact that when things look that way, we can expect such an outcome, may nonetheless be revealed by repeated expectation of the outcome in situation after situation when things in fact do look that way. While accepting something of the form "When things look F they are likely to turn G" our subjects' acceptance is manifest not through conscious articulation, but only through a pattern of "inferences."

And we come finally to the question "What might justify commitment to such an inference pattern?" Sundry things could do so. The fact that the pattern fits one's experience and is accepted in part at least because of that, for one thing. That's one way to block the threatening regress. Another way is simpler: namely, that we be innately hard-wired for that inference pattern, by God or Nature, so that it may justifiedly guide our reasoning. And this it might do even independently of whether the environment jibes with our specific cognitive makeup when we make that inference. The inference is still "justified" in any case, since it is the sort of inference appropriately made downstream from experience, regardless of the aetiology of that experience or the nature of the environment, and thus regardless of how reliable the belief may be relative to the environment within which it is acquired or sustained. So long as in our world it is a normally successful pattern, and it is no accident that we have acquired and sustain the commitment to its use (through God or evolution) with sensitivity to its validity, we may evaluate ourselves individually as "justified" in the beliefs acquired or sustained by means of that pattern, and evaluate the beliefs (the believings) themselves as thus justified on that basis.[6]

Note finally how, compatibly with this approach, we might still enjoy such (internal) justification even when victims of the evil demon. For, in considering whether we are thus justified, we evaluate ourselves and our proceedings *downstream from experience*, and such proceedings are evaluable positively even if they unfold in a demonic world, so long as the basis for evaluation is how likely it is that their like would put us in touch with the truth *in the environment wherein the evaluation is rendered*. After all, the environment that provides the basis for the evaluation is not the demon world but the

---

[6] But we must be clear that "validity" here is broader than just formal, logical validity, and includes also the kind of subjunctive (or tendency) validity that underwrites inferring that x is G from the perceived fact that it is F, a subjunctive (or tendency) validity that amounts to it being the case that anything that (in the relevant environment) were F would also be G (or that F things tend to be G). Even if ours is not the only sense one could reasonably assign to philosophers' terminology of "epistemic justification," moreover, it does seem one interesting such sense.

actual world inhabited by the evaluators who are considering, as a hypothetical case, the case of such a victim.[7]

V. Principles and Circularity

Reid joins the crowd accusing Descartes of vicious circularity (EIP 6.5; p. 631):

Des Cartes certainly made a false step . . . ; for having suggested this doubt among others, that whatever evidence he might have from his consciousness, his senses, his memory, or his reason; yet possibly some malignant being had given him those faculties on purpose to impose upon him; and therefore, that they are not to be trusted without a proper voucher: to remove this doubt, he endeavours to prove the being of a Deity who is no deceiver; whence he concludes, that the faculties he had given him are true and worthy to be trusted.

It is strange that so acute a reasoner did not perceive, that in this reasoning there is evidently a begging of the question.

In assessing this disagreement between Descartes and Reid it will be helpful first to reflect in general on what it is that makes circular reasoning vicious, when it is vicious.[8]

---

[7] Consider our implicit belief in Reid's principles and the like, or the habits and other implicit commitments that guide our intellectual conduct. These are perhaps not "dowstream from experience," and seem exceptions to our claim that assessments of epistemic justification are indirectly assessments of cognitive structures, mechanisms, and proceedings downstream from experience; but in any case much the same reasoning as above would still apply also to the evaluation of our implicit, Reidian belief-guiding commitments, which would still be intrinsic to the subject, and separable from the vagaries of her environment.

[8] Reid often supports one's harboring the first principles constitutive of various faculties, and argues that we may trust these simply because they come from God. But how does he obtain epistemic justification for believing that they are so derived? How in the end could he here avoid the sort of circularity that he finds in Descartes?

Reasoning is related epistemically to knowledge in two ways, corresponding to two sorts of knowledge, the reflective and the unreflective. The latter, "animal" knowledge, is concerned with the acquisition and sustenance of apt, reliable belief, whereas the former requires the belief to be placed also in a perspective within which it may be seen as apt.

Animal knowledge repels circularity for reasons that do not concern reflective knowledge. Beliefs about matters beyond the subject's skin, in particular, must be acquired through mechanisms connecting that belief with how it is out in the world. Essential circularity ill suits a stretch of reasoning for making that connection unaided, vitiating it as provider of animal knowledge. When reasoning circles back on itself essentially, it fails to connect its conclusion aptly with the world so as to make it a viable candidate for knowledge. What is distinctive of reflective knowledge is unbothered by such detachment, however, since reflective knowledge, while building on animal knowledge, goes beyond it precisely through integration in a more coherent framework. This it achieves via an epistemic perspective within which the object-level animal beliefs may be seen as reliably based, and thus transmuted into reflective knowledge.

Several are the ways to acquire our Reidian or other principles: through training or schooling, for example, or by noticing correlations then buttressed through deliberate testing. Alternatively, one might just pick them up through life experience, or through appropriate testimony. Some (especially the Reidian) may even turn out to be just innate mechanisms triggered in the way language acquisition is said to be triggered while vastly underdetermined by available evidence. Our experience-trusting habits of thought, where in normal circumstances we take our shape and color appearances at face value, seem largely of this sort.

Reasoning will yield animal knowledge only if it holds up with truth, aptness, and justification at every lemma on which it relies essentially in connecting its conclusion with relevant external reality. This is bound to depend on ultimate premises owed to some sort of perception, aided perhaps by memory. At this level essential reliance on circularity is plausibly prohibited, since mere circles of reasoning will fail properly to connect any conclusion with the world beyond the circle.

That is however compatible with one's being subject to no such prohibition when the objective is knowledge that will be reflective and not just animal. Having grasped how it is around us through connections involving the perception/memory/reasoning required for animal knowledge, further reasoning on that basis may enhance our conscious integration and explanatory coherence, lending epistemic virtue to our beliefs. There is no more vice in this circular procedure than in a case of visually-apparent-sprinkling /circles-in-puddles/pitter-patter-on-the-window-panes/car-wipers-wiping/umbrellas-up/felt-drops-on-one's-bare-arms /recalled-forecast, etc. There is nothing wrong with accepting various subarguments in such a case concurrently, believing the conclusion of each partly on the basis of the other beliefs used as premises. It *would* of course be bad to hold those subarguments concurrently *absent any connection with the relevant externalia.* Even when one holds the lot of them concurrently interlocked, however, *this does not imply that one holds them so detached.* (And a special, rational form of viciousness spoils attempts to reach conclusions about the contingent world around us through reasoning detached not only from the world beyond but even from those states and beliefs required as peripheral intermediaries for the desired connection with the world. Prominent among these states are the experiential states whose job it is precisely to mediate in that way between our contingent beliefs about the world around us and the world that they are about. Much circular reasoning would be defective in just that way.)

By using our various faculties and subfaculties, including those constituted by certain habits or other inferential patterns, we may reach a consciously reflective worldview distinguished by two features from the largely implicit framework that precedes it. Call that earlier framework of implicit commitments and other beliefs *framework FI*. Call the later explicit worldview *framework FE*. Two epistemically significant features may distinguish FE from FI: (a) that the earlier implicit "beliefs" are now explicit, and (b) that such consciousness-raising enables greater cognitive coherence, with member beliefs now more tightly integrated with other component beliefs, now visibly interrelated.

According to Reid, we can rationally acquiesce in the use of our God-given faculties that yield the beliefs and the very concepts by which we thrive individually and collectively. How can he regard himself as epistemically justified in believing that these faculties are God-given and accordingly truth-conducive? Is not his reasoning bound to be just as viciously circular here as Descartes' reasoning is alleged to be?

A way out for Reid, ironically akin to Descartes' own way, is to distinguish between *scientia* and *cognitio*, between reflective and unreflective (animal) knowledge. It is viciously circular to reach the Reidian worldview via reasoning that includes claims concerning faculty reliability—i.e., the various commitments constitutive of the operative faculties and subfaculties—while these very commitments also comprise the worldview thus arrived at. This is viciously circular if we conceive of the commitments/beliefs arrived at as identical with the commitments from which they are derived as conclusions. On behalf of Reid, we may now respond that the conclusions we reach are conscious, explicit beliefs, constitutive of an explicit, articulated worldview; and these are *not* quite the same as our implicit intellectual-conduct-guiding commitments, no matter how closely related they may be, and indeed even should they turn out to share the very same contents.[9]

VI. Still: How Are Such Principles Justified?

This question still remains, particularly if the relevant contents are general, contingent propositions. How can such a proposition be justified foundationally or immediately, as a "self-evident" universal or probabilistic truth? How can we sensibly allow ourselves justification for believing such a truth from the armchair, absent proper empirical inquiry into our actual contingent surroundings?

On behalf of Reid, I answer: What would make us justified is that we proceed in an epistemically appropriate and

---

[9] But the defense of Reid here would survive even if one granted that the "beliefs" at the end of the reasoning are indeed the same after all as the "beliefs" that serve as inputs to that reasoning. One could still defend such reasoning, so long as it results in conclusion beliefs that are somehow significantly *changed* from how they were as premises of that reasoning: for example, if the result is an explicitly conscious and integrated system of beliefs, this may be a valuable result of such "reasoning" despite the fact that the inputs to it involved the very beliefs, in implicit subconscious mode, that are now consciously integrated. This may still reasonably be regarded as a cognitively valuable result, adding some measure of cognitive virtue to the resulting beliefs.

desirable way, given the aims of systematic acquisition and retention of truth (especially truth that gives understanding), and that we do so not haphazardly but by our nature and in keeping with the nature of things, which makes us non-accidentally sensitive precisely to the "validity" of the inferential patterns constitutive of those faculties and their bundled implicit commitments. Further pleasing explanatory coherence would derive from an explanation of how we are thus attuned by nature with how things stand around us. And this last could be detailed more specifically in various ways, the two main competing options involving respectively (a) Divine Providence, and (b) natural evolution; either one would serve present epistemological purposes. Reid clearly took the first (as did Descartes). But, however the story is detailed at that level, the fact remains: humans are a certain way by nature, a way that, given our normal environment, furthers our epistemic aims of attaining truth and understanding, and does so with non-accidental sensitivity to the truth, including the subjunctive truth constitutive of the validity of our inferential patterns. So we can be assessed for whether our inbuilt mechanisms are operating correctly even if, unfortunately, we are in an abnormal environment relative to which those very mechanisms operate so as to take us away from truth and understanding. The main point is now straightforward: namely, that the mechanisms in question might include, and according to Reid do include, taking our sense experience at face value, and gaining access to the states of mind of our neighbors through beliefs instinctively prompted by the external, behavioral signs of such states. Et cetera.

Thus may we attain justification for the use of our basic faculties, for our "belief" in or implicit commitment to the various "first principles" adherence to which in practice is constitutive of such faculties. And this justification would remain even for victims of a Cartesian evil demon. Reasoning from such implicit commitments may eventually yield conscious awareness of your faculties and subfaculties, of their nature and how they fit you for cognitive success in your relevant normal environment. To a greater or lesser extent this would constitute a worldview that underwrites, with coherent understanding, your use of those faculties. Moreover, such conscious awareness of your intellectual makeup (your nature and second nature) might also aid its gradual improvement, as when you no longer take the sun to be (strictly) rising, no longer take the oar to be bent, no longer take the Muller-Lyer lines to be incongruent, and so on. You might no longer accept deliverances which earlier, however briefly or long, had been admitted without question.

Is that vicious? No more so here than it was for Descartes. Who could object to the use of our faculties resulting in such a worldview with its attendant coherence and yield of understanding? How plausible, surely, that the individual component beliefs should also gain epistemically by now being part of a more comprehensively coherent and explanatory establishment. When we judge them better justified, our assessment is relational, true enough, and indirectly dependent on intellectual surroundings involving the believer's operative cognitive virtue. But that is no more strange than is the evaluation of the archer's shot as skillful, which remains an evaluation of the shot itself, even if an indirect one dependent on factors involving the surroundings, and most of all the archer's operative skill.

Our Cartesian defense of Reid adumbrates the stance on virtuous circularity and reflective knowledge to be developed in Part II. But first let us consider what other options there may be, what other ways to surpass the sort of indirect realism and classical foundationalism found wanting in earlier chapters. Next we turn to Sellars' way, and after that to Davidson's.

Chapter 5
Mythology of the Given

I. How Does Experience Bear on Knowledge?

Central European analytic philosophy in the first half of this century focused on the relation between science and experience. Controversies extended beyond the philosophy of science, and shook philosophy to its foundations, affecting every part of the discipline: from aesthetics and philosophy of religion to metaphysics and epistemology. The issue of how experience relates to thought and language had two components: First, how does it relate to meaning? Second, how does it relate to knowledge?

Controversy raged over the empiricist criterion of meaningfulness, which set the positivists against all others but brought them together as their emblem. On the second issue, by contrast, they were divided. What is the epistemological bearing of experience on scientific knowledge? On this question Otto Neurath and Moritz Schlick had a famous controversy. According to Neurath, our ship of knowledge must be rebuilt at sea, and only its coherence really matters. This Schlick rejected, however, as "an astounding error." Schlick saw coherentism as adrift, and insisted on experiential moorings.

This controversy, though hardly novel with the Vienna Circle, much exercised them, and soon involved Rudolf Carnap and Carl Hempel and, eventually, Hans Reichenbach. With these it crossed the Atlantic, and with Karl Popper the Channel. Throughout much of the middle of the century it held center stage in epistemology.

It is this second issue that I would like to take up: What is the epistemological bearing of sensory experience on our knowledge?

II. Foundationalism

The idea of epistemically foundational status appears already in Carnap's *The Unity of Science* (1932), where a "protocol" statement is defined as a "direct record of a scientist's experience." A "primitive" protocol is then said to be one that *excludes* " . . . all statements obtained indirectly by induction or otherwise."

In the middle decades of the century, the doctrine of foundationalism took a radical form, a throwback to Cartesian epistemology. Schlick, for example, required indubitable and incorrigible foundations. Soon thereafter, C. I. Lewis also adopted that requirement, thus recanting his earlier "conceptualistic pragmatism."

Many others also adopted a radical foundationalism of certainty. "This doctrine," says Nicholas Rescher, "insists on the ultimate primacy of absolutely certain, indefeasible, crystalline truths, totally beyond any possibility of invalidation." But Rescher himself rejects the quest for absolute foundations as "quixotic."[1]

---

[1] *Methodological Pragmatism* (New York: NYU Press, 1977), p. 210. Rescher proposes to replace such foundations with "presumptions" accepted *prima facie*

Eventually a more moderate foundationalism is suggested by Hempel, who writes: "When an experiential sentence is accepted 'on the basis of experiential evidence', it is indeed not accepted arbitrarily; but to describe the evidence in question would simply mean to repeat the experiential statement itself. Hence, in the context of cognitive justification, the sentence functions in the manner of a primitive sentence."[2]

If put in terms of beliefs rather than sentences, Hempel's point appears thus:

(H) Beliefs held on the basis of direct experiential evidence are not arbitrary. Yet to state the evidence for such a belief is just to voice the belief. Hence, in the context of cognitive justification, these beliefs function as primitive or basic.

Roderick Chisholm credits Hempel for this insight, and makes it central to his own epistemology. Chisholm defends a form of foundationalism that admits apprehensions of the given at the foundation of empirical knowledge, and conceives of that foundation in line with Hempel's insight H.[3]

---

and subject to refutation. And he goes on to distinguish the rationality of practice from the rationality of theory, and to argue that the former permits a ". . . presumption in favor of established methods . . . [that] tilts the burden of proof in this context against a sceptical opponent" (p. 233). Rescher has developed this idea into an important version of pragmatism, but one that differs in kind from those I take up here.

[2] "Some Theses on Empirical Certainty," *Review of Metaphysics* 5 (1952): 621–9; p. 621. Carnap had spoken already in 1936 of the "confrontation of a statement with observation," and had proposed "acceptance rules" for such confrontation: "If no foreign language or introduction of new terms is involved, the rules are trivial. For example: 'If one is hungry, the statement "I am hungry" may be accepted'. . . . " (From "Truth and Confirmation," in Herbert Feigl and W. S. Sellars (ed.), *Readings in Philosophical Analysis* (New York: Appleton, 1949), p. 125. These claims appeared first in "Warheit und Bewährung," *Actes du congrès internationale de philosophie scientifique*, vol. 4 (Paris, 1936), pp. 18–23.

[3] In "The Theory of Knowledge," in *Philosophy: The Princeton Studies: Humanistic Scholarship in America* (Garden City, NJ: Prentice-Hall, Inc., 1964), Chisholm

Among the foundations defended by Chisholm, early and late, are sensory foundations—or apprehensions of the given—as well as knowledge of one's own beliefs and other propositional attitudes, which are also said to satisfy Hempel's conditions for being primitive or basic.

Such foundationalism was attacked famously by Wilfrid Sellars. Two main issues divided Sellars from Chisholm and fueled their long and widely followed controversy. Their disagreement involved, first, the relation of thought, or intentionality, to language, and, second, the relation of experience to empirical knowledge. On this second issue they thus continued the controversy of their predecessors from Central Europe: Neurath, Schlick, Carnap, and Hempel.

III. Foundationalism: For and Against

Sellars seems right in saying that Hempel's thesis points to inferences of the form:[4]

a) It is a fact that a is F;

So, it is reasonable (for me) to believe that a is F.

But his objection is now that any such argument as a will do its job only if the premise has authority, only if it is something which it is reasonable to believe. According to Sellars, this leads from β to the following alternative argument schema:

β) It is reasonable to believe it to be a fact that a is F;

So, it is reasonable to believe that a is F.

cites Hempel's work, and also an earlier paper by C. J. Ducasse, "Propositions, Truth, and the Ultimate Criterion of Truth," *Philosophy and Phenomenological Research* 1 (1939): 317–40.

[4] See Sellars' "Epistemic Principles," in his lecture series, "The Structure of Knowledge," in H. N. Castañeda (ed.), *Action, Knowledge, and Reality* (Indianapolis: Bobbs Merrill, 1975), pp. 337–8.

And this is of course, just as Sellars says, "obviously unilluminating."

That, again, is Sellars' critique. But the sort of problem he raises is not unique to his critique. A main theme of Richard Rorty's attack on foundationalism is the alleged "confusion of causation with justification" that he attributes to Locke and others. Donald Davidson also adds his voice:

> As Rorty has put it, "nothing counts as justification unless by reference to what we already accept, and there is no way to get outside our beliefs and our language so as to find some test other than coherence." About this I am, as you see, in agreement with Rorty.[5]

Just how damaging is that line of objection against experiential foundations? Doesn't it beg the question against Hempel's insight H? The insight, recall, is that certain beliefs have authority simply in virtue of being true. It is their *truth* that makes them reasonable. The believer thus becomes reasonable (or at least non-arbitrary) in so believing, simply because of the truth of his specific belief (which is of course not to say that any true belief would be equally reasonable since true). Therefore the believer does not need to employ any such reasoning as α or β. The believer does not need to adduce reasons in order to be reasonable in *such* a belief. That is indeed what makes it a *foundationally* justified (or reasonable) belief, according to Hempel. Inferential backing is here not needed. Truth alone is sufficient (given the belief's content).

---

[5] "A Coherence Theory of Truth and Knowledge," in Dieter Henrich (ed.), *Kant oder Hegel?* (Stuttgart: Klett-Cotta, 1983), reprinted in Ernest LePore, *Truth and Interpretation* (Oxford: Blackwell, 1986), pp. 307–20; p. 310. We shall examine Davidson's own approach in Chapter 6.

Hempel's insight hence appears to survive the sort of objection urged by Sellars, Rorty, and Davidson. But does it yield an acceptable foundationalism, as Chisholm believes? More specifically, does it adequately explain how it is that experience bears on knowledge? Shall we say that experientially given facts justify beliefs directly, merely through their truth? Shall we say, for example, that the mere fact that I have a headache suffices to justify my belief that I do?

What is the alternative to such foundationalism concerning how one is justified in believing that p? Circular or regressive reasoning will not adequately explain how that belief is justified. How could the belief that p derive its justification entirely from such reasoning? How, in either a pure regress or a pure circle, might justification ever enter in the first place? Inferential reasoning serves to transfer justification but this presupposes that justification is already there in the premises of the reasoning, and that is precisely what neither the pure circle nor the pure regress is able to explain. A full explanation of how one's belief that p gets to be justified must apparently take us back to ultimate premises that do not get all their justification from further premises yet. Must there not be ultimate premises that somehow get some of their justification by means other than reasoning from further premises? If not, it is hard to see how justification ever appropriately enters the line of reasoning (regressive or circular) that leads to one's being eventually justified in believing that p.

That sketches an argument in favor of the appeal to foundations. But mark well the highly determinable character of these foundations. All we have a right to suppose about our foundational beliefs, on the basis of our elimination of the circle and the regress, is that they are justified non-inferentially. Any more determinate and positive thesis would require further defense. In particular, we are in no position to conclude that the foundation must be constituted by direct apprehensions of the experiential given.

We have been considering how sensory experience bears on our empirical knowledge and justification. And we have found two opposing positions. On one side are Neurath, Sellars, Rorty, and Davidson, among others. According to this side, experience bears causally on our beliefs, but it is a serious mistake to confuse such causation with justification. Experience bears at most causally on our beliefs about external reality, even on our simplest perceptual beliefs. We do not *infer* such perceptual beliefs from beliefs about our sensory experience, nor is the justification for such beliefs a matter of their coherence with appropriate *beliefs* about our experience.

On the other side are Schlick, Hempel, C. I. Lewis, and Chisholm, among others. For these it is an "astounding error" to suppose that the mere coherence of a self-enclosed body of beliefs might suffice to confer justification on its members. And it is hard to see what, other than sensory experience, could serve to supplement coherence appropriately so as to explain empirical justification. Accordingly, they prefer rather to postulate beliefs about such experience, the takings or apprehensions of the given, through inference from which, or by coherence with which, one must attain one's empirical justification. But this side notoriously fails to find foundations contentful enough to found our rich knowledge of an external world.

IV. Some Middle Ground?

As so often in philosophy, this controversy leaves middle ground untouched. Our coherentists and foundationalists share an assumption:

(A) Experience can bear epistemically on the justification of belief only by presenting itself to the believer in such a way that the believer directly and non-inferentially believes it to be present, and can then use this belief as a premise from which to reach conclusions about the world beyond experience.

We can go beyond the traditional controversy by rejecting assumption A. Experience can bear epistemically on the justification of a perceptual belief *by* appropriately causing that belief.[6] Thus, while viewing a snowball in sunlight I may have visual experience as if I see something white and round, which may prompt the corresponding perceptual belief. In that case it will be an important part of what makes my perceptual belief epistemically justified—and indeed of what makes it a perceptual belief—that it is caused by such experience.

But does that serve to provide *foundational* justification for perceptual beliefs? Take a perceptual belief prompted appropriately by a corresponding experience. Take a belief that "this is white and round," one prompted by visual experience of a sunlit snowball in plain view. Is that perceptual belief *foundationally* justified simply in virtue of its causal aetiology? When Sellars inveighs against the Myth of the Given, he targets not only the radical version of the myth involving direct apprehensions of given experience. He objects also to the more moderate version that postulates foundational knowledge through perception. Indeed the key passage that encapsulates his opposition to a foundational epistemology targets not a foundation of introspective direct apprehension but a foundation of perception.

---

[6] Actually this sort of approach is defended already by Thomas Reid; see Chapter 3 above.

V. Sellars' Attack on the Myth of the Given

Here I avoid issues about the nature of thought and its relation to language and society. So I will take the liberty of transmuting Sellars' argument into one pertaining directly to belief, justification, and knowledge, leaving aside whether to understand these in terms of moves in a language game governed by social rules. I am not *denying* that our main epistemic concepts are to be understood thus in terms of language and society. I am simply not joining Sellars in affirming it. Thus my preference for the transmuted argument that does not prejudge these issues. So transmuted, here then is the Sellarsian refutation of the epistemology of foundations:

We have seen that to constitute knowledge, an observational belief must not only *have* a certain epistemic status; this epistemic status must *in some sense* be recognized by the person whose belief it is. And this is a steep hurdle indeed. For if the positive epistemic status of the observational belief that this is green lies in the fact that the existence of green items appropriately related to the perceiver can be inferred from the occurrence of such observational beliefs, it follows that only a person who is able to draw this inference, and therefore has not only the concept *green*, but also the concept of an observational belief that this is green—indeed the concept of certain conditions of perception, those which would correctly be called "standard conditions"—could be in a position to believe observationally that this is green in recognition of its epistemic status.[7]

---

[7] "Empiricism and the Philosophy of Mind," in H. Feigl and M. Scriven (eds.), *Minnesota Studies in the Philosophy of Science*, vol. I (Minneapolis: University of Minnesota Press, 1956), pp. 253–329. Reprinted in R. M. Chisholm and R. J. Swartz (eds.), *Empirical Knowledge* (Englewood Cliffs, NJ: Prentice-Hall, 1973), pp. 471–541; p. 512.

In arguing thus, Sellars is of course rejecting externalist reliabilism. It is not enough that an observational belief manifest a tendency to believe that one faces a green object "if and only if a green object is being looked at in standard conditions." This may give the belief a certain minimal epistemic status. But if the belief is to constitute real knowledge then " . . . this epistemic status must *in some sense* be recognized by the person whose belief it is." And this is the hurdle that Sellars regards as "steep indeed." It is this hurdle that in his eyes dooms foundationalism. If the hurdle is steep for the foundationalist, however, it seems no less steep for anyone else. How could anyone avoid the threatening circle or regress? How could one acquire the required knowledge about which conditions are standard, and the knowledge that those conditions are present, without *already* enjoying a lot of the observational knowledge the possibility of which is under explanation? Here now is Sellars' proposed solution (transmuted):

All the view I am defending requires is that no belief by S *now* that this is green is to count as observational knowledge unless it is also correct to say of S that he *now* knows the appropriate fact of the form *X is a reliable symptom of Y*, namely that the observational belief that this is green is a reliable indicator of the presence of green objects in standard conditions of perception. And while the correctness of this statement about Jones requires that Jones could *now* cite prior particular facts as evidence for the idea that such belief *is* a reliable indicator, it requires only that it is correct to say that Jones *now* knows, thus remembers, that these particular facts *did* obtain. It does not require that it be correct to say that at the time these facts did obtain he *then knew* them to obtain. And the regress disappears.[8]

---

[8] Ibid., p. 513. In the version of *Science, Perception, and Reality* published by Ridgeview Press in 1963, Sellars added the following footnote, on p. 169: "My

By this stage Sellars had highlighted inadequacies not only of traditional givenist foundationalism, but also of a more recent externalist reliabilism—a neat trick since, at the time he wrote, such reliabilism had not yet appeared in print. Nevertheless, Sellars' positive proposal is problematic. In the first place, how realistic is it to suppose that at the later time one remembers that the particular facts in question *did* obtain? Think of any perceptual knowledge that you can attribute to yourself now. Think, perhaps, of your knowledge that you are perceiving a rectangular sheet of paper with a certain pattern of marks on it. Is it realistic to suppose that, in believing perceptually that before you there lies such a sheet, you are relying on recollected incidents in which you succesfully perceived thus?

And there is a further problem. Our later access to earlier observational reactions is an exercise of memory. But memory itself seems to require, no less than perception, some meta-awareness of its reliability when exercised in circumstances of the sort in which it is now exercised.[9] And if there was a problem of regress attaching to the exercise of perception there would seem to be an equally disturbing problem of regress attaching to the exercise of memory. Perhaps the response would be that *just as* earlier proto-perceptions can become data supportive of generalizations about our perceptual reliability, generalizations that underlie later perceptual knowledge; *so, similarly,* earlier proto-memories can become data supportive of generalizations about our mnemonic reliability,

thought was that one can have direct (non-inferential) knowledge of a past fact which one did not or even (as in the case envisaged) *could* not conceptualize at the time it was present."

[9] This requirement is defended in my *Knowledge in Perspective* (Cambridge: Cambridge University Press, 1991), pp. 280 ff.

generalizations that underlie later mnemonic knowledge. Perhaps, but this raises even more poignantly an objection akin to that raised earlier about perceptual knowledge: namely, that we cannot plausibly be said to remember particular earlier exercises of memory constitutive of a data bank which can later support our underwriting generalizations.

VI. Sellars' Attack on Foundationalism: A Closer Look

At the heart of the Myth of the Given, Sellars finds this claim: that in making observation reports we are guided by prelinguistic takings of the given, whose authority our reports inherit. Finding this unacceptably obscure, Sellars prefers a kind of reliabilism. What gives epistemic authority to an observational report is said to be rather this: its manifesting the speaker's tendency to issue such reports if and only if he then observes the state of affairs described by the report (given, presumably, that the issuing of a report on that question is then called for).

If a report is to express knowledge, it must be responsive to its authority: *in some sense*, says Sellars, the speaker must recognize that authority. But this is "a steep hurdle indeed." For it implies that the speaker must know the likes of this: that his token reportings of the presence of something green are reliably related to the presence of something green. And how could one ever come to know such a generalization if in order to know of any positive instance one must *already* know the generalization?

This is the question that Sellars answers unconvincingly. He contends that eventually one may be able to remember having earlier seen instances of green while uttering "this is green," even if one did not know at that earlier time that one faced anything green. Evidently he hopes thereby to skirt the problem of vicious circularity, for one's generalization would then have a basis independent of any items *currently seen* to be green. Isn't it plain false, however, that our observational knowledge must always rest on some such generalization supported by a data bank of positive instances? Few perceptual reports stay long in memory. We soon forget even what was noticed conceptually at an earlier time. How plausible can it be that we now remember even what we did *not* notice, even some of what we *could* not have noticed, for lack of the requisite concepts?

Besides, there is the already bruited problem about memory. And there is a further problem about the power of combined memory and perception to deliver the epistemic goods. Memory-cum-perception is now supposed to deliver *direct* knowledge of what happened earlier—knowledge unmediated by inference—so it is itself a reporting faculty. "That *was* green," a report based on memory-cum-perception, seems then equally subject to our worries about color (green) perception. The authority of memory-cum-perception reports seems just as much a matter of our reliability in the circumstances standard for such reports. Can these reports express knowledge, so as to serve as data for a generalization about our reliability in such reports? In order for such memory-cum-perception reports to express knowledge, we must issue them in the knowledge that they are authoritative, which requires us to know that such reports tend to be right. But how could we get the prior data required for an inductive inference to any such general belief? We here face a mere variant of the earlier problem about perceptual knowledge of green items.

Sellars' reasoning now under scrutiny is taken by Michael Williams to concern not so much epistemology as semantics or philosophy of mind. He supposes it to be, not so much (i) an explanation of epistemic normativity, of what accounts for the authority of our observational reports, as (ii) an explanation of what is involved in the meaning of such reports or in the possession of certain contents by the beliefs that they express. He correctly stresses Sellars' holism, his idea that we gain meanings for our language and contents for our mind in networks, not through independent pairings that could stay in place whatever happened to our other pairings. Meanings and contents come in systems: you could not possibly retain just one word-meaning pairing even while losing everything else in your language. Accordingly, it is an empiricist fantasy to suppose that our knowledge is acquired seriatim, through instances of observational knowledge, leading eventually to a database for inductive conclusions about the reliability of our faculties of observation.[10]

Yes, Sellars is of course committed to that critique of empiricism, and may be giving expression to it in the relevant section of "Empiricism and the Philosophy of Mind," section VIII, on whether empirical knowledge has foundations. That section is also concerned, however, with the *epistemic* and not just the *semantic* standing of our observational reports. Even granted all the points about what it takes to acquire a language with meanings, and what is required for command of empirical concepts, including observational concepts, we still face this question: How can we gain justification for believing empirical, contingent generalizations about our

[10] M. Williams, "Mythology of the Given: Sosa, Sellars, and the Task of Epistemology," *Aristotelian Society Supplementary Volume* 77 (2003), pp. 91–112. My reply is "Human Knowledge, Animal and Reflective," ibid., pp. 113–30.

own perceptual reliability? We still need to see how we could possibly acquire epistemic justification for any such general, contingent belief (and not just how we gain a grasp of its content, or learn the words to express it). In that section Sellars is clearly dealing with this question of justification (or of "authority"), even if he is also dealing with semantics, and with the fixing of mental content.

Williams shows awareness of this: ". . . Sellars needs a view about the justification, as well as the semantic character, of non-inferential reports. In particular, he needs a view that allows him to distinguish semantic embedding from inferential dependence." This would seem to follow from the obvious fact that it is *possible* for one to have an *un*justified belief, and to voice it in a report. Even unjustified beliefs must have contents, even unjustified reports must have meaning. One can abide by all relevant semantic rules, so as to attain such meaning, such content, despite falling short of justification. What is required for epistemic correctness hence goes beyond observing any semantic rules, indeed beyond anything that gives us semantic correctness. How then does Sellars think we attain such extrasemantic epistemic correctness?

Williams offers two suggestions. First we are directed to Sellars' idea that a particular report may be justified ". . . as being an instance of a general mode of behaviour which, in a given linguistic community, it is reasonable to sanction and support."[11] Here Sellars opts for a kind of "rule utilitarianism" in epistemology, with his "general modes of behavior" taking the place of moral rules. This is at best a temporary waystation,

---

[11] W. Sellars, *Empiricism and the Philosophy of Mind* (Cambridge, MA: Harvard University Press, 1997) p. 74. The monograph was first published in Feigl and Scriven (eds.), *Minnesota Studies in the Philosophy of Science*, vol. I.

however, since it leaves us wondering what constitutes our being *reasonable* in sanctioning and supporting some such mode of behavior, what sort of thing is involved in our being thus reasonable. Confronted with this question, Sellars might well have issued one of his "promissory notes." Indeed, we shall soon examine the reasoning by which he might then have tried to make it good.

Sellars is also said to deal with issues of epistemic justification in a second way. "The sceptic," writes Williams,

. . . wants to know how anything whatsoever that we believe is justified. His suggestion is that, for all we know, *all* our beliefs might belong in a box with "rumours and hoaxes." Given Sellars's conception of meaning, this is not a worry to take seriously. Without an extensive system of beliefs, keyed in certain ways to direct observation, one would not be in the believing game at all. Having a lot of justified beliefs is a precondition of having any beliefs whatsoever.

How is this to be reconciled with Williams' own insistence that Sellars needs a view about the justification, as well as the semantic character, of non-inferential reports? Why suppose that we must have a *lot* of justified beliefs as a precondition of having any beliefs at all? Will this help us understand how our beliefs gain such justification? Can we be told more fully and explicitly what enables our beliefs to become thus justified, what this justification derives from?

Compare Davidson's argument that our sentences-believed-true must in the main *be true*, given the conditions required for them to have their meanings. Take our observation reports. Davidson's point is that they have the meaning they do because they are prompted by the presence of certain sensible characteristics in objects that we perceive. But they are also *about* these prompting situations. So they

must be largely true: if they were not, then they would not
be largely prompted as they are, in which case they would
not be about that, they would mean something else. Such
semantic considerations are then used by Davidson to deal
with a kind of skepticism. He needs to cross a gap from
"mostly true" to "default justified," however, which proves
a treacherous crossing. For one thing, Davidson would not
deny justification to ordinary people, and even philosophers,
innocent of Davidsonian semantics. How then do the semantics help ordinary folk attain their justification?[12] This
question is especially pressing if only beliefs justify beliefs. It
is thus increasingly obscure just how Sellars is supposed to
cross in one giant leap the gap that proves so treacherous
to Davidson. How do we get the result that our reports
and the beliefs they express must be largely enough justified
just as a logical consequence of our semantics? How is this
supposed to happen, if epistemic normativity goes beyond
semantic normativity, if even properly abiding by all semantic rules and regulations can still leave us short of epistemic
justification?[13]

[12] Compare Davidson, "Reply to Nagel," in the Davidson volume of the
Library of Living Philosophers, ed. Lewis E. Hahn (Chicago: Open Court,
1999):

Nagel quotes "A Coherence Theory of Truth and Knowledge" as saying, "The
agent has only to reflect on what a belief is to appreciate that most of his basic
beliefs are true." I was concerned to show that each of us not only has a basis for
his picture of the world in his perceptual beliefs, but that he also, on reflection,
would see that there was a reason (my arguments) for thinking this. I was trying to
fend off the criticism . . . that I might have shown that we do have a large supply
of true beliefs, but not have shown that these constitute knowledge. I now think
this attempt at fending off criticism was a mistake, if for no other reason than that
it would seem to credit only those whose philosophical thinking is correct with
knowledge.

[13] Davidson's own way with the gap will be the subject of Chapter 6.

VII. Sellars' Later Critique and Its Pragmatist Turn

In later work Sellars returns to his Myth of the Given, even quoting substantially from the earlier discussion. This later work implicitly concedes how misguided were those earlier attempts to find inductive backing for trust in the reliability of our belief-forming faculties. Indeed, it also manifests awareness of our problem for invoking access through memory-cum-perception to data from the past, that this just postpones the problem without solving it, since it raises the same issues. Nor does that later work rest content with any simple idea that "epistemology recapitulates semantics." And if the new work is compatible with the rule–utilitarian theme, it also takes a surprising, pragmatist turn.

Consider first some relevant passages.[14]

62. How, we are inclined to expostulate, could it be reasonable (at t) to accept [a theory T which coheres with our introspections, perceptions, and memories] *because* it is supported by our introspective, perceptual, and memory judgements (IPM judgements), if it is *because* they fall under [principles that affirm the reliability

---

[14] From Sellars' "More on Givenness and Explanatory Coherence" (first published in 1977), as reprinted in Jonathan Dancy (ed.), *Perceptual Knowledge* (Oxford: Oxford University Press, 1988). Compare Sellars' "Epistemic Principles" (first published in 1975), as reprinted in Ernest Sosa and Jaegwon Kim (eds.), *Epistemology* (Oxford: Blackwell, 2000), p. 132:

[Surely,] . . . it will be urged, facts about learning languages and acquiring linguistic skills are themselves empirical *facts*, and to know these facts involves perception, memory, indeed, all the epistemic activities the justification of which is at stake. Must we not conclude that any such account as I give of the principle that perceptual beliefs occurring in perceptual contexts are *likely to be true* is circular? It must, indeed, be granted that principles pertaining to the epistemic authority of perceptual and memory beliefs are not the sort of thing which *could* be arrived at by inductive reasoning from perceptual belief. . . .

of such IPM judgements] that it is reasonable to accept these IPM judgements? . . .

66. [What we are groping for is] . . . a way in which it could be *independently* reasonable to accept [such principles affirming the reliability of our basic faculties] in spite of the fact that a ground for accepting them is the fact that they belong to T, which we suppose to be an empirically well-confirmed theory. . . .

68. Such an . . . account might well be called 'Epistemic Evaluation as Vindication'. Its central theme would be that achieving a certain end or goal can be (deductively) shown to require a certain integrated system of means. For the purposes of this necessarily schematic essay, the end can be characterized as that of being in a *general* position, so far as in us lies, to *act*, that is, to bring about changes in ourselves and our environment in order to realize *specific* purposes or intentions. . . .

77. [Can] . . . one espouse theory T *for the reason that* it is inductively reasonable to do so, and be *reasonable* in so doing? We have already seen that the answer is 'No!'.

78. Clearly we must distinguish the question 'How did we get into the framework?' from the question 'Granted that we are in the framework, how can we justify accepting it?' In neither case, however, is the answer 'by inductive reasoning' appropriate. . . .

80. As to the second question, the answer, according to the proposed strategy, lies in the necessary connection between being in the framework of epistemic evaluation and being agents. It is this connection which constitutes the objective ground for the reasonableness of accepting *something like* theory T. . . .

83. Notice, then, that if the above argument is sound, it is reasonable to accept . . . IPM judgments are likely to be true, simply on the ground that unless they *are* likely to be true, the concept of effective agency has no application.

This principle, that IPM judgments are likely to be true, encapsulates Sellars' version of Roderick Chisholm's "epistemic principles," which for Chisholm specify how *justification* derives from various factors. In his detailed discussions of Chisholm's epistemic principles, something to which he returned again and again in his classes and in his writings on epistemology, Sellars identified judgments of ostensible introspection, perception, or memory as IPM judgments.[15] His Chisholm-inspired principles are formulated as follows:

T-I   Ostensibly introspective judgments (I judgments) are likely true.

T-P   Ostensibly perceptual judgments (P judgments) are likely true.

T-M   Ostensibly mnemonic judgments (M judgments) are likely true.

From T-I, T-P, and T-M we may of course derive:

T-IPM   Ostensibly introspective, perceptual, or mnemonic judgments are likely true.[16]

Here again we must be sensitive to the distinction between truth and justification so important in considering Davidson's way with the skeptic, and also Williams' account of Sellars' way. For Chisholm's principles would take a different form, as follows:

J-I   Ostensibly introspective judgments (I judgments) are justified.

---

[15] For Sellars' intense focus on Chisholm's epistemology, see also *The Metaphysics of Epistemology* (Atascadero, CA: Ridgeview Publishing Company, 1989), ed. Pedro Amaral, a record of Sellars' undergraduate course in epistemology.

[16] Such epistemic principles are the focus of his "Givenness and Explanatory Coherence," op. cit, and he discusses them in depth also in several other publications; for example, in one of his three Matchette Lectures at the University of Texas, published as "The Structure of Knowledge," in Castañeda (ed.), *Action, Knowledge, and Reality*; and also in his *The Metaphysics of Epistemology*, op. cit.

J-P   Ostensibly perceptual judgments (P judgments) are justified.

J-M   Ostensibly mnemonic judgments (M judgments) are justified.

From J-I, J-P, and J-M we may of course derive:

J-IPM Ostensibly introspective, perceptual, or mnemonic judgments are justified.

Compare Richard Foley's distinction between subjective and objective justification, which leads him to say this about Chisholm's principles:

Although I have qualms about the exact formulations of some of his principles, I also think that most of them have a general aura of plausibility. After all, most roughly expressed, what the principles imply is that in general it is rational for us to trust memory, perception, introspection, and the like, and of course most of us think that this is sound intellectual advice.[17]

In one important sense of rationality, it is rational to _____ if we have a goal X and if on suitably careful reflection we would think that _____ is an effective way to satisfy X. This applies to our epistemic goals as well as our other goals. Thus, it is in general rational for us to have beliefs that conform to Chisholm's principles, because in general Chisholm's principles, or at least something similar to them, reflect our own deep epistemic standards. They reflect our own deep views about how best to reach our primary intellectual end—that is, truth.[18]

Foley's distinction highlights a relation between Chisholm's J principles and Sellars' T principles. According to Foley, the

---

[17] Richard Foley, "Chisholm's Epistemic Principles," in *The Philosophy of Roderick Chisholm*, ed. Lewis E. Hahn (Chicago: Open Court, 1997): 241–65; pp. 261–2.

[18] Ibid., p. 263.

J principles reflect our deep commitment to the T principles. And now we have three interestingly different stances on the J principles.

First, one might with Chisholm take them to be wholly independent of the T principles.[19] Second, one might with Foley take them to be independent of the *truth* of the T principles, but dependent on our deep enough *acceptance* of them. Or, third, one might propose some further explanation of them, as does Sellars with his practical, vindicational justification of the T principles. I will very briefly suggest some doubts about each of these, and then sketch the further alternative that I find preferable.

About Chisholm's stance, one main problem is that it is very hard to see how a notion of "justification" or "rationality" or "reasonability" could matter in epistemology, in connection with knowledge, while *wholly* independent of truth. Even assuming this problem could be surmounted, another problem would remain: that the principles seem motley unless unified by some overall account of what they have in common, of what gives them their common point.[20]

[19] Thus consider his statement in the 3rd edn, of *Theory of Knowledge* (Englewood Cliffs NJ: Prentice-Hall, 1989), pp. 76-7): "According to [my, Chisholm's] ... traditional conception of "internal" epistemic justification, there is no *logical* connection between epistemic justification and truth. ... [But the externalist] feels that an adequate account of epistemic justification should exhibit *some* logical connection between epistemic justification and *truth*."

[20] In addition we would have to ask what makes it reasonable for us to accept Chisholm's epistemic principles. In his latest relevant discussion (*Theory of Knowledge*, 3rd edn.), Chisholm denies that they are justified a priori. But he also declares a faith important to epistemology: namely, the faith that (F) we can improve our epistemic situation by making our body of beliefs better justified. And he argues that the J principles *can* enjoy a sort of a priori status, at least indirectly. *Consider*, for each of them, the conditional having F as antecedent and that principle as consequent. For Chisholm such conditionals *are* justified a priori. Thus the following conditional (or some variant) would

About Foley's stance, it does provide a unifying connection to truth if only via the requirement of a deep commitment to the T principles, which speak of truth and not only of justification. This sense of justification, Foley-rationality, *is* plausibly epistemic. It amounts to conforming to one's own deep epistemic standards. But a believer might conceivably have standards that are epistemically quite deplorable no matter how deep, as would someone deeply committed to the dicta of astrology. But the point can also be made without recourse to what is only hypothetically so, in some remote possible world. Deepest standards for belief regulation in our *actual* world can have functions that bear less on truth than on solidarity and coordination, as with some primitive myths, which seem plausibly to require nothing short of belief if they are to serve their latent functions. Can it plausibly be supposed that it is nevertheless their sheer depth that gives the relevant standards epistemic efficacy. Surely there must be some further sense of justification that matters in epistemology. And it remains to be seen what principles might govern such further justification, and how these principles are to be defended.

Sellars argues that our reasons for accepting the T principles cannot be inductive, on pain of vicious circularity. The T principles cannot have a non-vicious defense through being part of a theory T whose support is ultimately that it coheres with IPM judgments. So he turns to a practical justification of the T principles, claiming that

. . . it is reasonable to accept . . .

[T-IPM] IPM judgments are likely to be true

be one we *can* know a priori: that *if* we can improve our epistemic situation *then* ostensibly perceptual judgments are justified. I discuss this approach in "Chisholm's Epistemic Principles," *Metaphilosophy* 34/5 (2003): 1–10 (containing proceedings of an APA memorial session).

simply on the grounds that unless they *are* likely to be true, the concept of effective agency has no application.[21]

But how could this explain our *epistemic* justification for accepting the T principles? We want effective agency, true enough, and it might be suggested that this somehow gives us reason to accept the T principles. Even *if* it does, however, it will not be *epistemic* reason.

Thus, if a foundation offers a big prize to those who can get themselves to believe the T principles, this gives a reason of sorts for doing so, but that would not help us with the traditional epistemic problematic. We would not thereby have found the right sort of reason, an epistemic reason, for accepting the T principles. In any case, the reason for my caution, for my "even if," is that it is not quite clear how Sellars' vindicational argument is supposed to go. His reasoning is not straightforwardly pragmatic, as would be the reasoning of those who might draw from the foundation's offer an argument for somehow adopting the now desired belief. The practical syllogism deriving from the foundation's offer is rather analogous to the sorts of pragmatic arguments for belief famously propounded by Pascal, for one, and William James, for another; and it may even be involved in Kierkegaard's writings on "subjective truth." But Sellars' argument seems dangerously more like a case of wishful thinking. Suppose we want X and realize we won't have it unless p. To suppose that this gives any reason to believe that p is to indulge in wishful thinking. And it is true that, in a more subtle and indirect way, wishful thinking does confer a kind of pragmatic advantage. That is to say, the thinking itself will fit together with one's desires so as to yield satisfaction,

---

[21] "Epistemic Principles," Para. 83.

in the way in which it is satisfying to believe that your wishes are satisfied or on the way to being satisfied, by contrast with the frustration in believing the opposite. Can this possibly be what Sellars has in mind?

Certainly not, but it is not easy to turn up a more plausible alternative. Sellars does make it explicit that T-IPM "is epistemically prior to the reasonableness of particular IPM judgements . . ." (at para. 86). Epistemically *prior*, he says, not posterior or even coordinate; but we are left wondering how then T-IPM acquires its epistemic standing. And if we say that it does so through some factor other than I, or P, or M, say factor E, of coming built into our brains through evolutionary design, then don't we simply have a further source now, namely source E, and don't we now face the same problematic, with an expanded cast of factors that includes now I, P, M, and E? Sellars does not confront this, and what he does say, about the "necessary connection between being in the framework of epistemic evaluation and being agents" is insufficiently developed. Consider the fact that we cannot act effectively unless our IPM judgments are reliable. Why should that fact give us an *epistemic* reason for thinking that our IPM judgments *are* reliable. This takes us back to pragmatic vindication, with its attendant problems.

It has been argued that it is the "principal message" of Wittgenstein's *On Certainty* that the sceptic is on to an insight missed by Moore: namely, ". . . that to be a rational agent pursuing any form of cognitive enquiry—whether within or outside one's own epistemic locality—means making presuppositions which—at least on the occasion—are not themselves the fruits of such enquiry and are therefore not known. . . . Since rational agency is not an optional aspect of our lives, we are entitled—save when there is specific evidence to the contrary—to make the presuppositions that we need to make in living out our conception of the kind of world we inhabit and the kinds of cognitive powers we possess."[22] This sort of account offers the most promising way to think of Sellars' vindicational strategy. However, deep skepticism attacks from within the very possibility of our being thus rational. Can it be a proper response to just lay down the premise that we simply are? Nor is it clear enough in what sense rational agency is not "optional." Does this mean that anyone alive is in fact a rational agent? Must anyone alive be a rational agent specifically with respect to their beliefs? Must one be a rational agent more specifically with respect to external world beliefs? If these questions have answers we still need to see them. Moreover, and perhaps most importantly: we still need to be shown how to cross the gap from "We must make *some* presuppositions *or others*," to "We are justified in making *these* presuppositions, whatever specific ones enable our knowledge of the external, of other minds, etc."

In any case, however more subtle may be the form of his vindicational argument, Sellars would seem subject to the objection that practical reasons yield no epistemic normative standing. And if the argument is that we can take our efficacy as agents as a premise from which to infer as a conclusion that our IPM judgments are reliable, how does this avoid the alleged vicious circularity of inductive support for such reliability?

An improved account of epistemic principles will need to find a proper connection between epistemic justification

<hr>

[22] From the penultimate paragraph of Crispin Wright's "Wittgensteinian Certainties," in D. McManus (ed.), *Wittgenstein and Scepticism* (London: Routledge, 2002).

and truth, without abandoning what is plausible in the requirement that one satisfy one's own deepest standards. We need to discriminate among standards, however, at least by requiring that the standards be true if they are to do the full epistemic job. It is not enough that the standards be *simply* true; even for the deepest standards, we need to distinguish between those that have and those that lack proper epistemic standing. But how might our basic epistemic T principles acquire such standing? Not just through ordinary induction; Sellars does seem right about that. But we need to go beyond Sellars' own "vindication," which fails to give *epistemic* standing, and also beyond Chisholm's epistemic faith, since, even while sharing it, we will want something epistemically more rewarding.

Where shall we look for this better way? In recent decades a powerful current has swept away the priority of the radically subjective, and has moved epistemology beyond the inner, the internal, the foundational, towards a view of the subject as embedded in fundamental ways within his social and natural environment. The mind is thus viewed as extended out into the world through its external contents. This enables a powerfully argued way to naturalize epistemology. Many have signed on to this externalization and naturalization movement. Among the earliest, most subtly, and deeply argued efforts is that of Donald Davidson. In part for this reason, we shall focus on his work, as representative of that broad current of thought.

Chapter 6

Epistemology Naturalized, Davidson's Way

Davidson's epistemology, like Kant's, features a transcendental argument as its centerpiece. Both philosophers reject any priority, whether epistemological or conceptual, of the subjective over the objective, attempting thus to solve the problem of the external world. For Davidson, three varieties of knowledge are coordinate—knowledge of the self, of other minds, and of the external world. None has priority. Despite the epistemologically coordinate status of the mind and the world, we are told, the content of the mind can be shown to entail how it is out in the world. According to Davidson, our beliefs could not possibly have the contents that they have, unless the world around us was pretty much the way we take it to be, at least in its general outline. We are thus offered a way to argue, to all appearances a priori, from how it is in our minds to how it is in the world. The argument is a priori at least in being free of contingent premises or assumptions about the world around us or our relation to it. From premises about the contents of our propositional attitudes, the argument wends its way to a conclusion about how the world around us is structured and populated.

Before presenting his own account, Davidson rejects received views of meaning and knowledge. What follows will combine themes from his critique of alternatives with his more positive account and its way with the skeptic.

I. Davidson's Epistemic Argument Against Empiricist Theories of Meaning

Empiricist accounts of meaning, including Quine's and Dummett's, lead to skepticism, warns Davidson, who sees an advantage of his own account in its better response to the skeptic. Why do the earlier accounts lead to skepticism? Why does his own account do better?

According to Davidson,

. . . Quine and Dummett agree on a basic principle, which is that whatever there is to meaning must be traced back somehow to experience, the given, or patterns of sensory stimulation, something intermediate between belief and the usual objects our beliefs are about. Once we take this step, we open the door to skepticism for we must then allow that a very great many—perhaps most—of the sentences we hold to be true may in fact be false. . . . Take Quine's proposal that whatever there is to the meaning (information value) of an observation sentence is determined by the patterns of sensory stimulation that would cause a speaker to assent to or dissent from the sentence. . . . Quine's proposal, like other forms of verificationism, makes for skepticism. For clearly a person's sensory stimulations could be just as they are and yet the world outside very different. (Remember the brain in the vat.)[1]

Just how is this supposed to substantiate the charge that rival theories of meaning lead to a radical skepticism about objective external reality? According to Davidson, those theories

---

[1] Donald Davidson, "A Coherence Theory of Truth and Knowledge," in E. Lepore (ed.), *Truth and Interpretation: Perspectives on the Philosophy of Donald Davidson* (Oxford: Blackwell, 1986), 301–19; p. 313.

open a logical gap between our subjectivity and objective externalia: that is to say, between intrinsic descriptions of the contents of our minds and contingent facts about the world around us. And we are then necessarily unable to close this logical gap (not, presumably, without vicious circularity).[2] These are central themes sounded repeatedly in Davidson's writings on epistemology. Consider, for example, this passage.

> There is at least a presumption that we are right about the contents of our own minds; so in the cases where we are right, we have knowledge. But such knowledge is logically independent of our beliefs about a world outside, and so cannot supply a foundation for science and common sense beliefs. This is how skeptics, like Hume, reason, and I think they are right: knowledge of the contents of our own minds cannot be the basis for the rest of our knowledge. If this is correct, then our beliefs about the world must, if they are to count as knowledge, stand alone. Yet it has seemed obvious to many philosophers that if each of our beliefs about the world, taken alone, may be false, there is no reason **all** such beliefs might not be false.[3]

Here we have two main points: first, that if external reality is logically independent of the contents of our minds, then the contents of our minds can give no foundation for our beliefs about that external reality. And there is also a second point. Even if no particular contingent empirical belief is guaranteed to be right, we may still be able to show how we cannot be generally wrong about the world around us. Despite universal

---

[2] Compare Nagel's discussion of Davidson's epistemology, "Davidson's New Cogito," *The Philosophy of Donald Davidson*, ed. Lewis E. Hahn (Chicago: Open Court, 1999), p. 203; we shall return to this passage below.
[3] Donald Davidson, "Epistemology Externalized," in *Subjective, Intersubjective, Objective* (New York: Clarendon Press, 2001), 193–204; p. 194.

fallibility in individual empirical beliefs, we might still secure a guarantee that our beliefs must be mostly right, that we are inevitably, massively right about the world around us.

The gap that yawns between our subjectivity and the external world, according to earlier views, is repeatedly blamed by Davidson as a source of radical skepticism. In his view such skepticism bedevils not only supernaturalist, classical foundationalists, such as Descartes, but also contemporary externalist, coherentist, naturalists: Quine himself, for example. What exactly is the argument for so surprising a pairing and so unexpected a charge? Given the interest and importance of this issue, we are fortunate to have it explained by Davidson himself with his customary pith, in an account worth quoting and considering in full:

According to Quine's "naturalized epistemology" we should ask no more from the philosophy of knowledge than an account of how, given the evidence we have to go on, we are able to form a satisfactory theory of the world. The account draws on the best theory we have: our present science. The evidence on which the meanings of our sentences, and all our knowledge, ultimately depend is provided a person with his only cues to "what goes on around him." Quine is not, of course, a reductionist: "we cannot strip away the conceptual trappings sentence by sentence." Nevertheless, there is according to Quine a definite distinction to be made between the invariant content and the variant conceptual trappings, between report and invention, substance and style, cues and conceptualization.

What matters, then, is not whether we can describe the data in a neutral, theory-free idiom; what matters is that there should be an ultimate source of evidence whose character can be wholly specified without reference to what it is evidence for. Thus patterns of stimulation, like sense-data, can be identified and described without reference to "what goes on around us." If our knowledge of the world derives entirely from evidence of this kind, then not only may our senses sometimes deceive us; it is possible that we are systematically and generally deceived.

It is easy to remember what prompts this view: it is thought necessary to insulate the ultimate sources of evidence from the outside world in order to guarantee the authority of the evidence for the subject. Since we cannot be certain what the world outside the mind is like, the subjective can keep its virtue—its chastity, its certainty for us—only by being protected from contamination by the world. The familiar trouble is, of course, that the disconnection creates a gap no reasoning or construction can plausibly bridge. Once the Cartesian starting point has been chosen, there is no saying what the evidence is evidence for, or so it seems. Idealism, reductionist forms of empiricism, and skepticism loom . . .

Instead of saying it is the scheme–content dichotomy that has dominated and defined the problems of modern philosophy, then, one could as well say it is how the dualism of the objective and the subjective has been conceived. For these dualisms have a common origin: a concept of the mind with its private states and objects . . .[4]

According to Davidson's reasoning, certain philosophical positions, Quine's for example, lead to skepticism by allowing a certain crucial possibility. In his study of Davidson's epistemological views, Thomas Nagel endorses this reasoning, and joins in taking the crucial "skeptical possibility" to be this: that the external world could differ radically despite presenting subjectively indistinguishable appearances; that a logical chasm divides our subjective appearances from the world beyond. By leaving that possibility open one smooths the way for the skeptic. Nagel reminds us of the many ways in which the skeptic has been opposed without success.

[4] Donald Davidson, "The Myth of the Subjective," in his *Subjective, Intersubjective, Objective* (New York: Clarendon Press, 2001), pp. 42–3.

One might try to refute him by reducing external reality to subjective experience, for example, which is the way of phenomenalists, verificationists, pragmatists, transcendental idealists, and internal realists. Reductionists deny that it is really possible for one's experience to remain indistinguishable even while external reality diverges as broadly as the skeptic imagines. And such reductionism is one traditional way in which philosophers have tried to oppose the skeptic.

An alternative option does not rely on any ontological reduction of the world to the mind. But it attempts to argue its way out from the internal to the external nevertheless, as did Descartes, for example, or in some other way.

According to Nagel, Davidson has a third way with the skeptic, one that attempts to relate the external to the subjective neither by deduction nor by reduction. Some might be misled to see it as an attempted reduction, not of the external to the subjective, but in the opposite direction. However, in fact Davidson is no reductionist at all, not in the way of the behaviorist, nor in any such way. Despite renouncing reductionism, Davidson still finds an a priori argument that we cannot be as radically mistaken about the external as the skeptic would have us believe. If the attempt succeeds, therefore, it does, amazingly enough, refute the skeptic, and does so from the armchair.

An a priori argument is said to be crucially required, since we cannot fall back on retail empirical beliefs in arguing against a radical skeptic. To appeal thus to empirical beliefs would just beg the question, since the skeptic puts in doubt all such beliefs in one fell swoop.

The a priori argument is needed because the empirical reasons for particular beliefs are not by themselves sufficient. It makes sense to think about each of a great many of my beliefs, taken one at a time, that it might be false, in spite of the evidence. Some reason must be given to show that these individual possibilities can't be combined into the possibility that most of them are false. That reason can't be just the sum of the particular reasons for each of them, since these are just further beliefs in the set, and the whole question is whether most of them might be false. If they were, their apparent support of one another would be systematically misleading. So we cannot demonstrate empirically that this is not the case, as is proposed by naturalized epistemology; it must be *proved* to be impossible if skepticism is to be ruled out. We need an a priori argument, and Davidson has given us one. It is an argument which does *not* rely on the reduction of truth to coherence.[5]

Davidson's response is to agree, effusively so, and even to reject the one gesture by which Nagel tries to distance him from any such purported a priori refutation of the skeptic.[6] Nagel had ventured that Davidson would resist viewing his reasoning as designed to run *from* thought *to* objective reality. In response Davidson counters by avowing his intention to argue in precisely that way. Davidson concludes his response with a caveat of his own, but one that would give Nagel no pause, nor much gladden the skeptic.

Nagel is understandably astonished that a priori reasoning should show that our general picture of the world around us "covering vast tracts of history, natural science, and ordinary lore," is largely true. Of course, as he notes, there is an empirical premise, the *cogito*. There is not an a priori proof that there is a world more or less as I think of it. Nor is the empirical premise a small one. The conclusion that I know that the world, both in general and in many particular ways, is as I think it is, depends on the fact that I have just the beliefs I do.[7]

---

[5] Nagel, "Davidson's New Cogito," *The Philosophy of Donald Davidson*, p. 203.
[6] See his "Reply to Thomas Nagel," ibid., pp. 207–9.
[7] "Reply to Nagel," p. 209.

Whether this removes the "a priori" character of the reasoning is a matter of definitional opinion. In what follows let us take reasoning to be "a priori" so long as it relies neither on any substantive commitments concerning the external world, nor on external observation as a mode of acquiring justified beliefs. Reasoning is thus not reduced from a priori status simply because it rests on contingent commitments concerning the contents of the reasoner's own mind. It is in this sense of "a priori" that Nagel had tried to distance Davidson from a priori reasoning designed to counter the skeptic. And it is taken in *this* sense that Davidson rejects that gesture.

Regardless of how we choose to speak, the substance of Davidson's claim will remain amazing anyhow. Who would have thought that, just on the basis of otherwise a priori reflection, reasoning from our knowledge of what we believe, of how it is within our own minds, we should be able to arrive at substantive conclusions about the objective and independent external world around us? This is indeed the sort of reasoning that Cartesians once attempted.

Nagel is not fully persuaded to join Davidson in arguing thus against the skeptic, but he does think that Davidson has come up with a deep paradox. The only ways out he can see are, first, a Platonism that is anathema to contemporary naturalism, and, second, a radical ". . . form of skepticism about whether one was really capable of significant thought."[8]

II. Skepticism About Davidson's Account of Skepticism

Let us concede for argument's sake the need for an a priori argument if we are to oppose the skeptic with any hope of

---

[8] "Davidson's New Cogito," p. 205.

success, just as Nagel supposes, about which Davidson seems to concur. Suppose even that Davidson *has* given us the sort of argument we need. Even so we are not much better off against the skeptic, and indeed such a concession would admit a skeptical Trojan horse, or so I will argue.

Consider an unfortunate victim of futuristic technology whose brain is wirelessly controlled by demonic controllers. Suppose this to have come about only hours ago, perhaps overnight while the victim slept soundly. *This* possibility Davidson's reasoning does not preclude. So now we face the following outcome. True, we cannot reason that we might be generally wrong just because we might be wrong in any specific instance. But nor can we reason that we are safe from being wrong in any specific instance just because we cannot be generally wrong. So even if Davidson's reasoning enables us to close the gap between what is accessible to us a priori and our general correctness about the character of external reality, this still leaves in place gaps aplenty between what is accessible to us a priori and the various specific substantive beliefs that we hold about the world and our place in it at any given time. None of these gaps would seem bridgeable just with an argument like Davidson's.

It might be argued that appearances are here deceptive, as they so often are in this dark swamp. After all, Davidson's argument does yield the conclusion that our substantive beliefs about externalia are and must be massively correct. May we not therefore conclude that any particular such belief must then have presumptive justification? Such justification might be defeated, of course, by particular untoward circumstances. Absent such defeat, however, it is certainly not nothing. And so we seem to have made progress against the skeptic after all.

This argument has a certain "blanketing" property that should give us pause. It would render all substantive beliefs presumptively justified, the astrologer's along with the astronomer's. And now the action would shift to what accounts for the difference, what accounts for the defeat of the astrologer's justification and the non-defeat of the astronomer's justification. Anyone who believes something out of the blue, and has no very good argument against his reliability on the subject matter involved, any trusting soul innocent of relevant theory, would seem to inherit undefeated epistemic justification.

What is more, there is a further problem that Davidson himself has come explicitly to recognize: namely, that if we are thinking of justification as provided by his proposed complex reasoning, then only those enlightened few who grasp and adopt that reasoning would have their knowledge protected against the skeptic. The masses of non-philosophers, indeed the masses of non-Davidsonians, no matter how brilliant and otherwise well informed, would remain benighted. In spite of this, Davidson retains hope that his account will still do some epistemic good. So we will need to consider how any such reasoning might accomplish its good work.

III. Davidson's Argument and the Skeptic's Trojan Horse

If we frame our debate with the skeptic as do Davidson and Nagel, the skeptic wins regardless of whatever success Davidson's transcendental argument may enjoy. The success of the transcendental argument turns on complex and still disputed issues in the philosophy of language and mind. Even if that should all turn out favorably, however, once we think of skepticism as suggested by the writings of Davidson and Nagel, there is no way ultimately to overcome skepticism. We are unwise if in effect we thus allow the skeptic to set the agenda and frame the issue. We should be wary of setting up the dialectic with the skeptic along the following lines, in the fashion often attributed to Descartes:

1. If we are to know realm W it must be via realm M.
2. The way to know a realm X via a realm Y is by knowing Y and reasoning validly from one's knowledge of Y to conclusions about X.
3. Only deductive reasoning is really valid.
4. There is a logical gap between M and W that no deductive reasoning could possibly bridge.

(Here M is the realm of one's mind at the given time, and W is the realm of one's surrounding objective world.)

However, one does not defeat the skeptic simply by rejecting 3, while also adding inductive reasoning to our set of valid forms of reasoning. For it is no more clear how to cross the gap between M and W through valid *inductive* reasoning. Once we grant a division such as that of M and W above, and concede that any knowledge of W would have to be via knowledge of M, it will be hard to withstand the attack of the skeptic.

On one straightforward reading, Davidson's way of framing skepticism puts the realm of one's beliefs B in place of the realm M of one's mind in the argument above. Accordingly he does inherit the problem of crossing a divide from the subjective to the objective. How then does Davidson propose that we reason our way from B to W?

The argument is presented in various forms in several places. It appears as follows in Davidson.

The action has centered on the concept of subjectivity, what is "in the mind." Let us start with what it is we know or grasp when we know the meaning of a word or sentence. It is a commonplace of the empirical tradition that we learn our first words (which at the start serve the function of sentences—words like 'apple', 'man', 'dog', 'water'—through a conditioning of sounds or verbal behavior to appropriate bits of matter in the public domain). The conditioning works best with objects that interest the learner and are hard to miss by either teacher or pupil. This is not just a story about how we learn to use words: it must also be an essential part of an adequate account of what words refer to and what they mean.

Needless to say, the whole story cannot be this simple. On the other hand, it is hard to believe that this sort of direct interaction between language users and public events and objects is not a basic part of the whole story, the part that, directly or indirectly, largely determine how words are related to things. . . . The grasp of meanings is determined only by the terminal elements in the conditioning process and is tested only by the end product: use of words geared to appropriate objects and situations. This is perhaps best seen by noticing that two speakers who "mean the same thing" by an expression need have no more in common than their dispositions to appropriate verbal behavior; the neural networks may be very different. The matter may be put the other way around: two speakers may be alike in all relevant physical respects, and yet they may mean quite different things by the same words because of differences in the external situations in which the words were learned. . . ; in the simplest and most basic cases words and sentences derive their meaning from the objects and circumstances in which they were learned. A sentence which one has been conditioned by the learning process to be caused to hold true by the presence of fires will be true when there is a fire present; a word one has been conditioned to be caused to hold applicable by the presence of snakes will refer to snakes. Of course very many words and sentences are not learned this way; but it is those that are that anchor language to the world. . . .

The fallout from these considerations for the theory of knowledge is (or ought to be) nothing less than revolutionary. If words and thoughts are, in the most basic cases, necessarily about the sorts of objects and events that cause them, there is no room for Cartesian doubts about the independent existence of such objects and events. Doubts there can be, of course. But there need be nothing we are indubitably right about for it to be certain that we are mostly right about the nature of the world. Sometimes skepticism seems to rest on a simple fallacy, the fallacy of reasoning from the fact that there is nothing we might not be wrong about to the conclusion that we might be wrong about everything. The second possibility is ruled out if we accept that our simplest sentences are given their meanings by the situations that generally cause us to hold them true or false, since to hold a sentence we understand to be true or false is to have a belief. Continuing along this line, we see that general skepticism about the deliverances of the senses cannot even be formulated, since the senses and their deliverances play no central *theoretical* role in the account of belief, meaning, and knowledge if the contents of the mind depend on the causal relations, whatever they may be, between the attitudes and the world. This is not to deny the importance of the actual causal role of the senses in knowledge and the acquisition of language, of course.[9]

This passage contains the following main points:

1. [Interest-Guided Conditioning through which we acquire language] is not just a story about how we learn to use words, but must also be an essential part of an adequate account of their meaning and reference [their semantic properties].

[9] Davidson, "The Myth of the Subjective," pp. 43–5.

2. Direct interaction between language users and public events and objects is a basic part of what determines how words are related to things [and acquire their semantic properties].

3. In the simplest and most basic cases [the cases that "anchor language to the world"] words and sentences derive their meaning [and hence, for Davidson, truth conditions] from the objects and circumstances in which they are learned.

4. There need be nothing we are indubitably right about for it to be certain that we are mostly right about the nature of the world.

5. If words and thoughts are, in the most basic cases, necessarily about the sorts of objects and events that cause them, there is no room for Cartesian doubts about the independent existence of such objects and events.

6. The possibility that we might be wrong about everything is ruled out if we accept that our simplest sentences are given their meanings by the situations that generally cause us to hold them true or false.

In the simplest cases, we are told, words and sentences derive their meanings from the objects and circumstances in which they were learned. Just how does this happen? What sort of "derivation" is here in play? In leading up to and defending his "derivation" thesis, Davidson makes some revealing claims (which are quoted as follows, with my emphases in bold):

. . . [T]wo speakers who "mean the same thing" by an expression need have no more in common than their **dispositions to appropriate verbal behavior**; the neural networks may be very different. (p. 164)

A sentence which one has been **conditioned by the learning process to be caused to hold true by the presence of fires** will be true when there is a fire present; a word one has been conditioned to be caused to hold applicable by the presence of snakes will refer to snakes. (p. 164)

If words and thoughts are, in the most basic cases, necessarily about **the sorts of objects and events that cause them**, there is no room for Cartesian doubts about the independent existence of such objects and events. (pp. 164–5)

In considering this, and the many other passages where Davidson makes the same basic points, we need to distinguish between (a) dispositions to appropriate verbal behavior, and (b) the process or processes that may cause such dispositions in a certain speaker/believer. The disposition that one hosts in being such that "one is caused to hold a certain sentence true by the presence of fires," may have been put in place by repeated experience of fires. If so, that is just a contingent matter of fact, however, which might possibly have been otherwise. The actual disposition involves the fact that one *would* be caused to say or think "Fire!" in the presence of a fire (an evident enough fire). This most likely was indeed put in place through some experience by the speaker/thinker with actual fires. Even if that is so, it would seem only a contingent matter of fact, and the disposition might even have been there innately. But now we have a problem for Davidson's transcendental argument. For there is no evident impossibility in one's understanding the concepts of our commonsense objective reality, where this understanding resides, at least partly, in one's complex dispositions to verbal and other relevant behavior, although one has *not* acquired such dispositions through causal intercourse with exemplars of the concepts possessed.

So it seems at best unestablished that *both* (a) one could possibly have the beliefs that one has only through having in one's possession the concepts constitutive of the contents of those beliefs, and also (b) the only way one could have such concepts is through causal intercourse with their exemplars. Further defense would seem required in favor of assumption (b), for there is a plausible argument against it, one indeed suggested already by Davidson's actual words. It can be argued plausibly, after all, that the relevant requirement for possession of a concept, say, a recognitional concept, is only one's hosting a disposition that makes for differential sensitivity to the presence or absence of exemplars. And such a disposition *need not* have been acquired through causal interaction with actual exemplars.

IV. Davidson's Epistemology Naturalized

There are indications that Davidson has come to regard his argument as less plausibly a priori than one might have thought, perhaps even less so than he himself originally may have thought. Consider this recent passage:

Is my argument for the "massive" (essential) truth of our perceptual beliefs transcendental? If you accept the steps that lead to my version of externalism, . . . then you cannot, I think, be a skeptic about the existence of an external world much like the one we all believe we share, nor about the existence of other people with minds like ours. But the considerations in favor of semantic realism seem to depend in part not on purely a priori considerations but rather on a view of the way people are.[10]

---

[10] Davidson, "Reply to A. C. Genova," *The Philosophy of Donald Davidson*, p. 194.

Indeed, in recent passages Davidson candidly reveals his vacillation about epistemology and skepticism, especially in his more recent thought. The following are particularly revealing:

I have vacillated over the years on how to describe my attitude toward scepticism. Do I think that if I am right about the nature of thought scepticism is false, or that scepticism simply cannot get off the ground? Passages Stroud quotes suggest the former. At the same time, I have been happy to go along with Rorty in telling the sceptic to get lost. The two poses can be reconciled by pointing out that though I think scepticism as Stroud formulates it is false, I did not set out to show this. Reflecting on the nature of thought and interpretation led me to a position which, if correct, entails that we have a basically sound view of the world around us. If so, there is no point attempting, *in addition*, to show the sceptic wrong.[11]

Nagel quotes "A Coherence Theory of Truth and Knowledge" as saying, "The agent has only to reflect on what a belief is to appreciate that most of his basic beliefs are true." I was concerned to show that each of us not only has a basis for his picture of the world in his perceptual beliefs, but that he also, on reflection, would see that there was a reason (my arguments) for thinking this. I was trying to fend off the criticism (which perhaps surfaces in Stroud's contribution to this volume) that I might have shown that we do have a large supply of true beliefs, but not have shown that these constitute knowledge. I now think this attempt at fending off criticism was a mistake, if for no other reason than that it would seem to credit only those whose philosophical thinking is correct with knowledge. The right thing to say is rather this: we are *justified* in taking our perceptual beliefs to be true, even when they are not and so when they are true, they constitute knowledge (this is what

[11] Davidson, "Reply to Barry Stroud," *The Philosophy of Donald Davidson*, p. 163.

I meant by saying our perceptual beliefs are "veridical"). But since our only reasons for holding them true are the support they get from further perceptual beliefs and general coherence with how we think things are, the underlying source of justification is not itself a reason. We do not *infer* our perceptual beliefs from something else more foundational.[12]

In these passages we are given to understand that there is a source of justification other than the adducing of a reason for one's belief, or the basing of one's belief on a reason. Reason-based justification is not the sort of justification that Davidson calls to our attention in his many reflections about the bearing of his content externalism on issues of skepticism and epistemology. He has now seen this clearly, and acknowledges it openly. The source of justification that he focuses on is not a *reason*, inasmuch as it is a source of

---

[12] Davidson, "Reply to Nagel," p. 208. Compare his "Reply to McDowell":

My view is that particular empirical beliefs are supported by other beliefs, some of them perceptual and some not. Perceptual beliefs are caused by features of the environment, but nothing in their causality (except in special, derivative cases) provides a reason for such belief. Nevertheless, many basic perceptual beliefs are true, and the explanation of this fact shows why we are justified in believing them. We know many things where our only reasons for believing them are further beliefs. (pp. 105–6)

"A Coherence Theory of Truth and Knowledge" had taken a rather different view of the matter:

What is needed to answer the skeptic is to show that someone with a (more or less) coherent set of beliefs has a reason to suppose his beliefs are not mistaken in the main. What we have shown is that it is absurd to look for a justifying ground for the totality of beliefs, something outside this totality which we can use to test or compare with our beliefs. The answer to our problem must then be to find a *reason* for supposing most of our beliefs are true that is not a form of *evidence*. (p. 314)

I have not been concerned with the canons of evidential support (if such there be), but to show that all that counts as evidence or justification for a belief must come from the same totality of belief to which it belongs. (p. 319)

justification that epistemically favors even those who have no *belief* in any Davidsonian theory about how our beliefs and sayings acquire content.[13] Nor need one have any reason at all for beliefs that are nonetheless somehow justified. Again, nothing in the causality of perceptual beliefs provides a reason for them, while still ". . . many perceptual beliefs are true, and the explanation of this fact shows why we are justified in believing them." Those innocent of a Davidsonian account of the nature of mental content and meaning, would lack any rationale deriving from any such Davidsonian theory of content, in favor of their empirical beliefs about their environing world. But, if Davidson's account is true, they would still have a source of justification involving the nature of such content. And it is the existence and nature of such justification that Davidson now sees himself as having clarified through his writings on externalism, knowledge, justification, and skepticism.

The Davidsonian justification at issue is *not*, therefore, of either of the sorts that Nagel distinguishes. It is not a justification that derives from a reduction of the external to the subjective (or, for that matter, the other way around), nor from a deduction of the external from the subjective. Nor is it a justification that comes with possession of an argument, an *a priori* argument, through which one gains support for its conclusion. Davidson has concluded that it is hopeless to suppose that this is how people generally avoid the clutches of the skeptic. For people generally adduce no such Davidsonian argument in support of their retail beliefs.

[13] Compare this: "Perceptual beliefs are caused by features of the environment, but nothing in their causality (except in special, derivative cases) provides a reason for such beliefs. Nevertheless, many basic perceptual beliefs are true, and the explanation of this fact shows why we are justified in believing them." ("Reply to McDowell," pp. 105–6.)

So, even if a few philosophers, persuaded by Davidson, do adduce such a complex argument concerning the nature of mental and linguistic content, and even if they do *thereby* gain some measure of justification for their empirical beliefs, that will not explain the justification that ordinary folk have for *their* empirical beliefs, and so it will not explain how it is that *these folk* are safe from the objections of the skeptic.

What then *is* the source of the distinctive Davidsonian empirical justification that a subject's perceptual beliefs get from something other than the support of other empirical beliefs hosted by that subject. Apparently it is simply the *truth* of the Davidsonian account of how our sayings and attitudes must derive their content, and how this guarantees that one's picture of the environing world *must* be massively correct, especially in its perceptual components.

Two fascinating questions ensue. First of all, isn't Davidson now drawing on externalist, and indeed reliabilist intuitions? It would seem to be the high level of reliability of our empirical beliefs, given his account of meaning and content, that now serves as the core of the special source of justification invoked to explain the high epistemic status of our empirical, and especially of our perceptual beliefs.[14]

The second interesting question concerns the status of Davidson's theory and his "answer" to the skeptic. If the source of justification should now be viewed as distinct from any reasoning, from any invoking of a justifying argument, then it is no longer clear why it must be *a priori*. (Not that it was all that clear in any case.) It becomes positively opaque why the *a priority* of Davidson's epistemologically effective

---

[14] That at a deep level Davidson is a reliabilist is suggested already in my " 'Circular' Coherence and 'Absurd' Foundations," in Ernest Lepore (ed.), *Truth and Interpretation* (Oxford: Blackwell, 1986); see especially pp. 395–7.

reasoning should be an issue. Now it would seem to matter only that the reasoning establish the theory, for it is just the *truth* of the theory that has turned out to be epistemologically effective. What seems to matter is essentially that as things in fact stand in our contingent circumstances, content is set externalistically through causal linkages with our external environment. For it is through this fact that the reliability of our beliefs is assured. And it is from their assured reliability that their presumptive justification derives. Of course, if in no possible world could content derive in any other way, then the reliability of our beliefs would be assured with alethic necessity. But it is far from clear that Davidson's account, or any such content-externalist account, is true with alethic necessity.

Note, finally, that through this new approach we have a way to understand epistemology naturalized that avoids the objection, voiced for example by Nagel, that such naturalization of epistemology would involve a vicious circularity. This is also reminiscent of the longstanding controversy as to whether Descartes' supernaturalization is similarly vicious in its circularity. Consider how interesting in this connection is Davidson's new reason-avoiding approach, on which justification derives somehow from a source other than the subject's actual reasoning. As we have seen, the new approach strongly suggests a reliabilism for which justification can derive from the reliability of the sorts of beliefs at issue (perceptual beliefs most importantly, though Davidson also generalizes beyond these eventually). And Descartes' epistemological reasoning can be viewed similarly as proposing a way of understanding our forming of beliefs (in the lap of an epistemically benevolent God) as bound to be reliable. (Of course, for special reasons, Descartes *did* aim for alethic necessity, and for *a priori* reasoning, but the present comparison is independent of that.) For if Descartes' epistemological theorizing is meant to identify a way in which our beliefs get to be justified which is precisely *not* through any reasonings from which we derive them as conclusions, then Descartes too can avoid vicious circularity by responding to the skeptic that our beliefs' source of justification need not involve the use of reasoning. In Descartes' case the effective fact would involve assent attendant on sufficiently clear and distinct perception, while favored by God's epistemic benevolence. In Davidson's case the effective fact would involve rather that we would not form beliefs having the contents of our empirical beliefs did we not interact appropriately with surroundings characterized generally as are our surroundings in this world.

The main remaining question concerns the epistemic status of our empirical beliefs once we have reasoned along with Davidson, while leaning presumably on adequate empirical support. Do our empirical beliefs gain any epistemic status through such reasoning? It might be thought that obviously they do not. How could they do so without vicious circularity? How could such theoretical beliefs as to the nature of content add to the status of one's empirical beliefs generally, if it is granted that the theoretical beliefs must in turn gain their own status through reliance on empirical, perceptual beliefs?

Here again the comparison with Descartes is instructive. Descartes did obviously think that by the end of the *Meditations* he had improved himself epistemically. But it is hard to see how he could possibly have avoided the vicious circularity of which he has so often been accused. Since Descartes, early in the *Meditations*, puts so much in doubt, including even

his simplest arithmetical and geometrical beliefs, it is hard to
see how he could possibly dig himself out of so deep a skeptical hole while avoiding vicious circularity. Descartes does
have a way out, however, one also open both to those who
defend common sense, as does Moore, and to those who ad-
vocate an epistemology naturalized, either Quine's, or, now,
perhaps, Davidson's. The response is indeed a kind of "coherence theory of knowledge" after all, in line with Davidson's
famous title. For it is by adding interestingly to the coherence
of one's picture of the world and one's place in it that one is
able to gain a *further* measure of distinctive, epistemically valuable justification for one's own empirical beliefs, a measure
of justification that goes beyond the mere reliability of those
beliefs, a reliability we can see to follow from how we must
acquire contents and form beliefs. The additional measure of
justification goes beyond any delivered by sheer reliability,
and does so by bringing to consciousness a well founded
account of how our nature and emplacement yield such reliability. Whether this is done in the way of Descartes, or in
that of Moore, or of Quine, or, now, of Davidson, the result
would be, structurally, the same: a more satisfyingly coherent
account of our nature and place in the scheme of things.

PART II

Chapter 7

Human Knowledge, Animal and Reflective

I. Varieties of Human Knowledge

Human knowledge has at least two varieties, the animal and the reflective: 'knowledge' sometimes means the first, sometimes the second. This is not necessarily to say that the word itself is ambiguous in English. Perhaps the distinction is made through contextual or pragmatic devices that draw on the context of discussion. In any case, animal knowledge does not require that the knower have an epistemic perspective on his belief, a perspective from which he endorses the source of that belief, from which he can see that source as reliably truth conducive. Reflective knowledge does by contrast require such a perspective. Here now is a *necessary* condition for knowledge of either sort. Since the details will not matter, our formulation is rough and partial but sufficient unto the day:

(VR) A belief amounts to knowledge only if it is true and its correctness derives from its manifesting certain cognitive virtues of the subject, where nothing is a cognitive virtue unless it is a truth–conducive disposition.

VR is more closely adequate as an account of animal than of reflective knowledge. This is because reflective knowledge requires a specific *further* condition, namely perspectival endorsement of the reliability of one's sources. Let us step back for some perspective on these two varieties of knowledge, the animal and the reflective.

II. Epistemic Values and Why Knowledge Is a Matter of Degree

Knowledge seems a matter of degree in more than one respect. Here are four candidates:

(a) how sure one is about the matter known,
(b) how safe or unsafe is one's belief, how easily one might have been wrong,
(c) how rationally justified one is in so believing: e.g., how strong one's evidence is, and
(d) how reliably truth-conducive is the way in which one acquires or sustains one's belief.

When we say that, of two people who know something, one knows it better than the other, we may invoke one or more of these dimensions, especially the latter three. A belief is of higher epistemic quality if it is safer or more rationally justified, since based on better evidence, or more reliably acquired or sustained. When they constitute knowledge, the safer, better justified, and more reliably acquired beliefs constitute better knowledge. One knows some things better than other things.

Several epistemic values stand out:

(a) Truth: we would rather our beliefs were true than not true, other things being equal.

(b) Safety: we would prefer that not too easily would our beliefs be false.

(c) Understanding/explanation: often we would like not only to know a given thing, but also to understand it, to have an explanation. (And this leads to the next item.)

(d) Coherence: we would prefer that our minds not house a clutter of mere facts sitting there loose from one another.

(e) Finally, we are often interested not only in *having* the truth but in *discovering* it, which involves not just being visited with the truth by sheer happenstance or through some external agency, but to arrive at the truth through our own intelligent doings, by relying on our own reliable abilities, skills, and faculties.

We also evaluate our beliefs in other ways. We would like beliefs that are *useful*, for example. But this is not a cognitive category, unlike the earlier five.

Desiring by nature to know, people want more than just to get it right. What else, then, might be involved in the epistemic value of one's knowledge? Plausibly, the values distinguished above would all play some role. Here I leave open the question of whether the nature of coherence, and of understanding/explanation, requires explanation in terms of reliability in the actual world. Even if such explanation would be required at bottom, it may still be that coherence is a distinctive value with its own special status.[1] Elsewhere

---

[1] This is essentially the same issue as that of whether John Stuart Mill can preserve the purity of his utilitarianism while making a distinction between higher and lower pleasures. I argue that he can in "Mill's Utilitarianism," *Mill's Utilitarianism*, ed. James M. Smith and Ernest Sosa (Belmont, CA: Wadsworth Publishing Company, 1969), pp. 154–72. That we need to understand coherence and its

I argue that, absent reflective knowledge, one would miss a desirable respect of coherence and understanding, and its correlative sort of epistemic coherence.

To sum up: Virtue Reliabilism is true both for animal and for reflective knowledge. Prominent among values of the higher, reflective level is that of understanding. It is in part because one understands how one knows that one's knowing reaches the higher level. A belief constitutive of reflective knowledge is a higher epistemic accomplishment if it coheres properly with the believer's understanding of why it is true (and, for that matter, apt, or true because competent), and of how the way in which it is sustained is reliably truth-conducive. Cohering thus within the believer's perspective is, moreover, not irrelevant to a belief's being deeply attributable to the believer's epistemic agency. Guiding one's thinking with sensitivity to the truth would seem to involve some perspective on how one is forming and sustaining one's beliefs. Of course one knows plenty through one's animal nature, sans rational agency; which is how we know some of the things we know best. Even when one could take charge, finally, as a deliberative rational agent, it may be best to proceed on automatic pilot. But we do often take pride in grasping the truth through its deliberate pursuit, which hence is also valued as a positive accomplishment.

III. Is True Reflective Knowledge Beyond Our Reach? Cartesian Reflections

Can humans aspire to that higher level of knowledge, reflective knowledge, governed by this Principle of the Criterion:

value in terms of reliability is concluded in my "The Coherence of Virtue and the Virtue of Coherence: Justification in Epistemology," *Synthese* 64 (1985): 3–28.

PC *Knowledge is enhanced through justified trust in the reliability of its sources?*[2]

This is meant in the first instance as a principle about the contents of a single instance of consciousness at a given time when one actually considers the reliability of one's sources for a given conscious belief. But it can also be extended to cover one's implicit beliefs, which rise to the higher level only by meeting the requirement that under the light of reflection one must be able to defend the reliability of one's sources. Beyond unreflective, animal knowledge, therefore, humans aspire to a higher, reflective knowledge, which obeys our principle of the criterion.

Reflective knowledge has an important role in Descartes' epistemology. Early in the Meditations, he is struck by some troubling consequences of our "principle of the criterion," which may also be put as follows:

High-level knowledge requires justifiedly taking one's sources to be reliable.[3]

Recall his desire to counteract doubt that one's operative sources or faculties might be unreliable—thus the doubts deriving from the fallibility of the senses, from the possibility that one is dreaming, or is a victim of an evil demon, etc. The problem in each case is that one's belief might be unreliable: that is, might not with sufficient reliability protect one from error. And mark well Descartes' reaction: in order to remove such doubts, he wishes to establish that our beliefs do derive

---

[2] I have defended such a principle repeatedly; for example, in "How to Resolve the Pyrrhonian Problematic: A Lesson from Descartes," *Philosophical Studies* 85 (1997): 229–49. More fully stated, the principle holds the epistemic quality of one's belief to rise with justified awareness of the reliability of one's sources.

[3] A principle best relativized to those who grasp (understand) the proposition that they know that p.

from sources reliably worthy of our trust. This might be thought to follow from his aim to prove the reliability of our sources, without implying that we attain true knowledge only once we achieve that aim. How that misinterprets Descartes' intentions comes out in a crucial passage (quoted earlier already, but worth having before us in the present context once again):

The fact that an atheist can be "clearly aware that the three angles of a triangle are equal to two right angles" is something I do not dispute. But I maintain that this awareness of his [*cognitionem*] is not true knowledge [*scientia*]. . . . Now since we are supposing that this individual is an atheist, he cannot be certain that he is not being deceived on matters which seem to him to be very evident (as I fully explained). And although this doubt may not occur to him, it can still crop up if someone else raises the point or if he looks into the matter himself. So he will never be free of this doubt until he acknowledges that God exists.[4]

Principle PC sufficiently explains why Descartes will not be satisfied with unqualified foundationalism. Enlightened, reflective *scientia* requires the satisfaction of PC, and will not be attained through mere external foundations in the dark, not even when the foundational source is "internal" and as reliable as rational intuition is said to be.

Descartes will not settle for mere *cognitio*, not even for internalist, a priori, reason-derived *cognitio*, as attained by the *atheist* mathematician. Descartes wants *reflective, enlightened* scientia. It is *this* that sets up the problem of the Cartesian Circle.

---

[4] This passage is from the Second Set of Replies as it appears in *The Philosophical Writings of Descartes*, ed. J. Cottingham, R. Stoothoff, and D. Murdoch (New York: Cambridge University Press, 1984), vol. II, p. 101. Where this translation says that an atheist can be "clearly aware," Descartes's Latin is *clare cognoscere*.

Since Descartes wants not just reliable, truth-conducive *cognitio*, since he wants the enlightened attainment of reflective *scientia*, he needs a defense against skeptical doubts that target his intellectual faculties, not only his faculties of perception, memory, and introspection, but even his faculty of intuitive reason, by which he might know that $3 + 2 = 5$, that if he thinks then he exists, and the like. He thinks he can defend against such doubts only by coherence-inducing theological reasoning yielding an epistemic perspective on himself and his world, through which he might confidently trust his faculties. And these faculties must include those employed in arriving, via a priori theological reasoning, at his perspective on himself and his world, the perspective that enables confidence in the reliability of those very faculties.[5]

We may explicate Descartes's project by placing it in the context of the Pyrrhonian problematic. This also helps explain why the circle is virtuous, and how certain stages of the Cartesian project, seemingly incoherent at first blush, are defensibly coherent in the end. (Example: the apparently incoherent claim about needing to first prove the veracity of God.)

IV. Descartes and the Pyrrhonian Problematic

One question remains pertinent: What could possibly give to reflective knowledge a higher epistemic status than the

---

[5] There is a telling analogy, not explicitly recognized by Descartes, between the role of dreams in his skepticism vis-à-vis perception, and a role assignable to paradoxes and aporias in a parallel skepticism vis-à-vis rational intuition. That dreams are miscast in the drama of skepticism is the burden of chapter 1 of my *A Virtue Epistemology: Apt Belief and Reflective Knowledge, Volume I*(Oxford: Oxford University Press, 2007).

corresponding unreflective cognitio(n)? And, more particularly, what could possibly do so within the epistemological framework favored by Descartes?

What favors reflective over unreflective knowledge? Reflective acquisition of knowledge is, again, like attaining a prized objective guided by one's own intelligence, information, and deliberation; unreflective acquisition of knowledge is like lucking into some benefit in the dark. The first member of each pair is the more admirable, something that might be ascribed admiringly to the protagonist, as his doing. And we can after all shape our cognitive practices, individually and collectively, enhancing their epistemic virtue, their enabling us to grasp how matters stand. We can do so at least to some extent, which does not require that our every belief be freely chosen and deliberate. A tennis champion's "instinctive" reactions at the net derive from highly deliberate and autonomously chosen training carried out voluntarily over a period of years. Even when already in place, moreover, such "instinctive" reactions are still subject to fine-tuning through further practice and training. The same is true of a bird watcher and his binocular-aided "instinctive" beliefs. And the same is true of us all and our most ordinary visual beliefs, aided by the tutelage of daily practice and, eventually, the hard lessons of diminishing acuity.[6]

---

[6] It must be granted, however, that Descartes' *cognitio*-level attainments are importantly different from the grasp of gold by luck in the dark (an analogy from Sextus to which we shall soon return). The latter is more like a gambler's lucky guess. Undeniably, that distinction can and should be made. But it brings to the fore the fact that epistemic luck can be found at different levels and in different ways. Take a case where the gold-searcher enters a dark room that in fact happens to contain only gold objects, though he has no idea of this. Or take a case where there are several rooms before him, any of which he might enter, all dark and only one containing gold objects. If he happens to choose that one while ignorant of the relevant facts, again it is no accident in one respect that he lays hold of

A further advantage of reflective knowledge is its entailed increment of comprehensive coherence, something accepted by Descartes himself as a source of epistemic worth, indeed as a source of certainty. In Principle 205 of his *Principles of Philosophy*, for example, he notes that if he can make coherent sense of a long stretch of otherwise undecipherable writing by supposing that it is written in "one-off language," with the alphabet all switched forward by one letter, etc., the fact that he can make sense of the passage through that interpretation supports the hypothesis that it is correct. There he defends his account of physical reality in that " . . . it would hardly have been possible for so many items to fall into a coherent pattern if the original principles had been false."

Since the propositions that form the coherent pattern are "deduced" from the "original" principles, therefore if the coherence of the implicands signifies the truth of the principles, it likewise, derivatively, signifies the truth of the implicands themselves forming the pattern. Descartes seems therefore here again, as elsewhere, to be adopting a kind of reliabilism in defending the epistemological power of coherence—its ability to impart certainty—by appeal to its reliability as a source of the truth of what renders it certain.[7]

---

some gold, but it remains an accident in another respect. The Pyrrhonian gold-in-the-dark example can, I believe, be supplemented interestingly in the ways indicated, so as to support the intuition that one needs a reflective perspective rich and powerful enough to rule out more than just the weak possibility that one's belief is just as much a matter of blind luck as is a gambler's lucky guess.

[7] This appeal is also found at the heart of Descartes' epistemology, when in the second paragraph of the third Meditation he writes: "Certainly in this first knowledge there is nothing that assures me of its truth, excepting the clear and distinct perception of that which I state, which would not indeed suffice to assure me that what I say is true, if it could ever happen that a thing which I conceived so clearly and distinctly could be false." Reliability is hence assumed to be at least necessary in an acceptable source of epistemic status. A belief is supposed to be

Admittedly, in that same Principle (205) Descartes claims only *moral* certainty for his coherence-validated beliefs about the alphabet or about the natural world. However, in the very next principle (206) he claims *more* than moral certainty for his scientific principles, and does so, again, at least in part through appeal to explanatory coherence (when he adduces that they " . . . appear to be the only possible explanations of the phenomena they present").

Ancient skepticism, as represented by Pyrrhonism, and modern skepticism, as presented by Descartes, have been regarded as radically different. How plausibly? One problem raised by Descartes *is* limited by comparison with the radical skepticism of the ancients: namely, the problem of the external world. But this is not the only skeptical problem of interest to Descartes. It is obvious in the *Meditations* that his concerns are much broader, as when he wonders how he can know the truth even when he adds three and two or when he considers how many are the sides of a square. I have argued that it is precisely the radical skepticism of the ancients that mainly concerns Descartes (and not only Hegel, who is emphatic on the point). Moreover, this skepticism is best seen in the light of the epistemic problematic found already in Aristotle's *Posterior Analytics*,[8] where it is given a foundationalist resolution,

---

certain if one is assured of it by its clearness and distinctness, which requires that clearness and distinctness be a (perfectly) reliable guarantor of truth. Note well: it is the clearness and distinctness of the perception that *itself* yields the certainty, at least in the first instance. What yields the certainty is *not* just an argument that *attributes* in a premise clearness and distinctness to one's perception of what one is led to accept as a conclusion of that argument. (As we have seen, such an argument may *boost* the epistemic status of one's belief in its conclusion, by making it a case of reflective *scientia*. But that belief already enjoys the highest level of certainty attainable as a state of *cognitio* simply through the perception of what it accepts with sufficient clearness and distinctness.)

[8] A 3.

and, more famously, in the five modes of Agrippa. To the latter incarnation of that problematic the Stoics, in kinship with Aristotle, offer a foundationalist response. Where Aristotle appeals to rational intuition as a way to found scientific knowledge, the Stoics appeal to natural, animal perception as a way to found ordinary empirical knowledge.

Pyrrhonians reject such externalism because it dignifies mere "groping in the dark" with the title of knowledge. They favor *enlightened* knowledge, which requires awareness of one's epistemic doings. Only this is "knowledge" worthy of the title. Sadly, they would prefer in their own practice to suspend judgment in specific case after specific case, partly because they reject blind foundations. In their view, moreover, any attempt to move beyond foundations only misleads us into circles or regresses, viciously either way.[9]

Descartes' response is balanced and sensitive to this (Pyrrhonian) dialectic. It grants the truth in foundationalism by allowing an inference-independent epistemic state of *cognitio*. Perception, for example, might well give us such unreflective animal knowledge unaided by inference. Even intuition might give us foundational *cognitio*, a sort of unreflective knowledge open even to the atheist mathematician.

V. Epistemic Externalism

Externalist epistemologies have prompted much controversy. Internalists reject them as unworthy of human epistemic dignity. Externalism is denigrated as a "thermometer" model of

---

[9] The exceptions allegedly allowed by the Pyrrhonians, perhaps ordinary beliefs generally, as opposed to the theories of philosophers or scientists, would seem unmotivated if their best and deepest arguments would allow no such exceptions.

knowledge inadequate to the full complexity of human cognition.[10] Already, among the ancients, Pyrrhonians oppose the externalism of Galen and the Stoics. Sextus, in particular, invokes similes that illuminate our issue, such as the following:

Let us imagine that some people are looking for gold in a dark room full of treasures. . . . None of them will be persuaded that he has hit upon the gold even if he *has* in fact hit upon it. In the same way, the crowd of philosophers has come into the world, as into a vast house, in search of truth. But it is reasonable that the man who grasps the truth should doubt whether he has been successful.[11]

Most would not disdain the good fortune of striking it rich in the dark, but it is no doubt a lesser state than that of finding gold through a deliberate plan aided by good eyesight in clear light. Enlightened discovery is more admirable than is any comparable luck that may reward groping in the dark. For one thing, enlightened discovery is success attributable to the agent; luck in the dark is not.[12]

Suppose that, concerning a certain subject matter, you ask yourself whether you know, and you have to answer either "Definitely not," or "Who knows?" If so, then in some straightforward and widely shared sense surely you do not *really* know?

[10] Cf. Wilfrid Sellars' "Empiricism and the Philosophy of Mind," in H. Feigl and M. Scriven (eds.), *Minnesota Volumes in the Philosophy of Science*, vol. I (Minneapolis: University of Minnesota Press, 1956), section 36 of part VIII ("Does Empirical Knowledge Have a Foundation?"), which we examined in Chapter 5.

[11] *Against the Mathematicians*, VII. 52, in the Teubner text, ed. H. Mutschmann (Leipzig, 1914).

[12] In harmony with this Pyrrhonian sentiment, Confucius says in his *Analects*, bk. 2, no. 17: "To say that you know when you know, and to say you do not when you do not, that is knowledge."

Similarly, suppose that, concerning a certain choice or action of yours, you ask yourself whether it is right and you have to answer "Definitely not," or "Who knows?" Isn't there some sense in which your action or choice *thereby* falls short?

Such considerations may amount to nothing more than this: It is better to believe and to act in ways that are *reflectively* right than in ways that happen to be right but unreflectively so. There is a higher state of knowledge, reflective knowledge, but one subject to our Principle of the Criterion, PC above. Attaining such knowledge requires a view of ourselves—of our beliefs, our faculties, and our situation—in the light of which we can see the sources of our beliefs as reliable enough (and indeed as perfectly reliable if the *scientia* desired is absolute and perfect).

Why is such reflective *scientia* better than unreflective *cognitio*? First, because it is reason-molded, at least in the way of a champion's "instinctive" play. Second, because a knowledge that enjoys the support of a comprehensively coherent and explanatory worldview is better. But is it *epistemically* better? Is it better with a view to getting at the truth? That Descartes would respond affirmatively even here is made plausible by key passages in which he explicitly recognizes the epistemic power of explanatory coherence. In this, as in so much else within the core of his epistemology, he was right, and ironically ahead of the times whose epistemological temper was to be set by a widespread misreading of his thought.

In sum, Descartes was a foundationalist, *and* a coherentist, *and* a reliabilist. His form of reliabilism appears already early in the Third Meditation, where he says that clarity and distinctness could hardly serve as a source of certainty if it could ever happen that something could be so clear and distinct while false.

VI. The Pyrrhonian Predicament: More on the Way Out

Recall Descartes' commitment, already in the second paragraph of the Third Meditation, to the requirement that nothing as clear and distinct as is the *cogito* could possibly be false, if that degree of clarity and distinctness is to be what gives the *cogito* its status of certain knowledge. Recall also his observation that an atheist mathematician does not need to block the skeptical doubts of the *Meditations* in order to have a kind of knowledge of his mathematics, with a status that Descartes calls *cognitio*. Nevertheless, above the *cognitio* available to the atheist even absent a coherent meta-perspective, there is said to be a *scientia* that does require such reflective standing. What could possibly provide such standing? Cartesian answer: the ability to defend one's commitments in the arena of reflective reason. Yes, but through what standards, under what epistemic principles? And how do these standards or principles themselves acquire proper standing?

Even the deepest epistemic standards must fit coherently in one's overall body of beliefs and commitments, but must *also* connect properly with the reality to which they pertain. To connect thus properly, they must at least be true, as is the principle that the clear and distinct is infallibly true. What is more, our present commitment to them must not be right just by accident. When and how do we relevantly avoid such accident in our deep standards or principles? A good answer to this question should help explain just how it is that belief in epistemic principles can itself acquire epistemic standing.

According to Descartes' insight, it is *not* only through ordinary inductive inference that one could possibly hope to provide epistemic grounding for epistemic principles.[13] It is not only thus that one could relevantly escape debilitating luck in one's commitment to the principles. It may help that one be systematically and stably enough benefited by a powerful and benign enough Creator (or a provident enough Mother Nature), a possibility exploited by Descartes, in a way to be considered below. The epistemic benefits will compound, moreover, if, compatibly with our epistemic predicament, we manage to ascend to a full enough perspective on its true nature.

I have repeatedly been led to suggest in earlier chapters that this better solution thus takes us back, ironically, to a philosopher long miscast as the archetypal foundationalist and givenist. It is, I have suggested, in Cartesian epistemology that we find a way beyond our regress or circle. Descartes first meditates, with the kind of epistemic justification and even "certainty" that might be found in an atheist mathematician's reasonings, one deprived of a worldview within which the universe may be seen as epistemically propitious. His reasoning at that stage *can* be evaluated, of course, just as can an atheist mathematician's reasoning. After all, atheist mathematicians will differ in the worth of their mathematical reasonings. Absent an appropriate worldview, however, no such reasoning can rise above the level of *cognitio*. If we persist in such reasoning, nevertheless, eventually enough pieces may come together into a view of ourselves and our place in

---

[13] And here I mean epistemic T principles that specify how reliable are various ways of forming beliefs. Recall our discussion in Chapter 3.

the universe that is sufficiently comprehensive and coherent to raise us above the level of mere *cognitio* and into the realm of higher, reflective, enlightened knowledge, or *scientia*.[14] No circle vitiates that project.[15]

The Cartesian problem of the external world is much more restricted than the Pyrrhonian problem of whether we know anything at all. But the *Meditations* explicitly concerns not just the restricted problem but also the quite general Pyrrhonian issues. There can be no doubt that Descartes is in the same tradition as the ancient skeptics. Anyone who thinks that Hegel's focus on the ancients is a sharp departure from the moderns cannot have read Descartes closely. In this dialectic, the foundationalism favored by Aristotle and by the Stoics is rejected by the Pyrrhonians because, in their view, it dignifies

---

[14] And once any claims of priority are dropped, as I am proposing, then it might well be held that *cognitio* that p *and cognitio* that one enjoys *cognitio* that p, are both required for *scientia* that p. It might even be held that *scientia* that one has *scientia* that p is also required for *scientia* that p—so long as one concurrently entertains the proposition that one has scientia that p. So a form of the KK Principle seems accessible along this avenue.

[15] Among the pieces that need to come together in order to raise the belief that p above the level of *cognitio*, to the level of *scientia*, may well be found appropriate *cognitio that* one enjoys *cognitio* that p. Here's an objection I have received: that comprehensiveness and coherence are matters of degree while it is very hard to see how to draw a line above which lie the degrees of comprehensiveness and coherence that suffice for knowledge, though it was also suggested that we might do better by appealing to practical considerations and not just to comprehensiveness and coherence. However: (a) it is not clear how appeal to practical considerations will really help with the problem of drawing a line. Moreover: (b) compare a concept like that of being tall. That is presumably to be defined in some such way as this: being sufficiently taller than the average. Presumably someone just infinitesimally taller than the average is *not* tall. One has to be taller than the average by some margin, one has to be "sufficiently" taller than the average. But how do we define that margin? Is there, even in principle, some way to capture our *actual* concept of tallness by means of some such definition? There seems no way. Yet we do surely have and use a concept of tallness, do we not? Why can't we view epistemic justification similarly in terms of "sufficient" comprehensiveness and coherence?

"groping in the dark," by allowing foundational sources of epistemic status to operate in the dark, out of view.

By allowing an inference-independent epistemic state of *cognitio*, Descartes makes room for the insights of such foundationalism. Intuition gives us foundational *cognitio*, as suggested by Aristotle, and such unreflective knowledge is open even to the atheist mathematician. There is however a higher state of knowledge, reflective knowledge. Attaining such knowledge requires a view of ourselves—of our beliefs, our faculties, and our situation—in the light of which we can see the sources of our beliefs as reliable enough (and indeed as perfectly reliable if the *scientia* desired is absolute and perfect).

It is important to recognize, in assessing this Cartesian strategy, that while we do need to underwrite, at the later stage, the reliability of our faculties, what enables us to do so is the appropriate use of those very faculties in yielding a perspective from which reality may be seen as epistemically propitious. But we need not restrict ourselves to the use of rational intuition and deduction as the only faculties of any use in that endeavor. Descartes himself surely needed memory as well. And memory, by definition, operates over time. It is not a present-time-slice faculty. Nor, indeed, is deduction itself such a faculty, except where the whole proof can be seen in a flash. So memory, as a *cognitio*-level mechanism can join *cognitio*-level intuition and perception in yielding the pieces that, once present with sufficient comprehensiveness and coherence, can boost us to the level of reflective *scientia* able to underwrite all such faculties. This means that we need not later exhume from memory any particular cases of reliable perception or reliable memory in order to support inductively the generalizations about the reliability of our faculties. It is enough that such generalizations

be present because of the combined operation of past perception and memory (and, *perhaps*, a gradual "induction" over
time, and/or appropriate innate principles). If through such
cognitio-level cognitive processing enough of a coherent and
comprehensive picture comes together, such a picture can
still underwrite the continued use of those very faculties, now
with reflective assurance, and now at the level of enlightened
scientia.[16]

We have gone beyond the mythology of the given, first by
rejecting the assumption that experience can bear on the epistemic justification of our beliefs only by providing premises
yielding knowledge of a world external to experience. Here is
a better way to think of the epistemic efficacy of experience.
Visual experience as if this is white and round may cause
belief that this is white and round in the absence of any special reason for caution. That can yield perceptual knowledge
that this is white and round, with no need to postulate any
inference from one's experience to what lies beyond. *Maybe*
there are such inferences, lightning inferences unconsciously
or subconsciously yielding our perceptual beliefs as conclusions. But we need not enter that issue. It is enough that
experience cause belief in some appropriate, standard way.
Whether it does so via a lightning, unconscious inference
we can leave open. Whether it does so or not, it may still

[16] The combination of coherence and comprehensiveness comports with a
concept of epistemic justification that is "internal." But it remains to be seen just
where to draw the relevant boundaries: At the skin? At the boundaries of the
"mind"? At the present-time-slice? At the boundaries of the subject's lifetime?
Using some combination of the above? If so, which? And why? And why do
we and should we care whether people are thus "internally" justified? My own
answers would rest on a *subject-centered* conception of epistemic justification as
intellectual virtue, and on the importance to a social species of keeping track of
the epistemic aptitude or ineptitude of oneself and one's fellows, especially where
it is possible to exercise some measure of control, however indirect.

endow the perceptual belief with appropriate epistemic status to constitute perceptual knowledge.

Nevertheless, a mere thermometer reaction to one's environment cannot constitute the best human knowledge, regardless of whether that reaction is causally mediated by experience. It is not enough that one respond to seeing white and round objects in good light with a "belief" or "proto-belief" that there is something white and round. Suppose one asks oneself "Do I know that this is white and round?" or "Am I justified in taking this to be white and round?" and one has to answer "Definitely not" or even "Who knows? Maybe I do know, maybe I don't; maybe I'm justified, maybe I'm not." In that case one *automatically* falls short, one has attained only some lesser epistemic status, and not any "real, or enlightened, or reflective" knowledge. The latter requires some awareness of the status of one's belief, some ability to answer that one does know or that one is epistemically justified, and some ability to defend this through the reliability of one's relevant faculties when used in the relevant circumstances. But this leads to a threat of circle or regress, a main problematic, perhaps *the* main problematic of epistemology. Surprisingly, already in Descartes himself, in the founder of modern epistemology, we find a way beyond that problematic.

Chapter 8

Philosophical Skepticism and Externalist Epistemology

I. Philosophical Skepticism

We consider the following thesis and its supporting argument.

Philosophical Skepticism

There is no way we could ever attain full philosophical understanding of our knowledge.

The Radical Argument

A1. Any theory of knowledge must be internalist or externalist.

A2. A fully general internalist theory is impossible.

A3. A fully general externalist theory is impossible.

C. Therefore, *philosophical skepticism* is true.

In discussing these, first it will be convenient to define some terminology. 'Formal internalism' shall stand for the doctrine that a belief can amount to knowledge only through the backing of reasons adduced as premises. For short let's speak of 'internalism', but this is of course a very special sense of the word. Nevertheless internalism in our sense has long enjoyed substantial support. Here are some representative passages, drawn from the writings of Donald Davidson, Richard Rorty, Laurence BonJour, and Michael Williams.

[Nothing] . . . can count as a reason for holding a belief except another belief.[1]

[It] . . . is absurd to look for . . . something outside [our beliefs] . . . which we can use to test or compare with our beliefs.[2]

[Nothing] . . . counts as justification unless by reference to what we already accept, and there is no way to get outside our beliefs and our language so as to find some test other than coherence.[3]

[We] can think of knowledge as a relation to propositions, and thus of justification as a relation between the propositions in question and other propositions from which the former may be inferred. Or we may think of both knowledge and justification as privileged relations to the objects those propositions are about. If we think in the first way, we will see no need to end the potentially infinite regress of propositions-brought-forward-in-defense-of-other-propositions. It would be foolish to keep conversation going on the subject once everyone, or the majority, or the wise, are satisfied, but of course we *can*. If we think of knowledge in the second way, we will want to get behind reasons to causes, beyond argument to compulsion from the object known, to a situation in which argument would be not just silly but impossible. . . . To reach that point is to reach the foundations of knowledge.[4]

To accept the claim that there is no standpoint outside the particular historically conditioned and temporary vocabulary we are presently using from which to judge this vocabulary is to give up on the idea that there can be reasons for using languages as well as reasons within languages for believing statements. This amounts to giving

---

[1] Donald Davidson, "A Coherence Theory of Truth and Knowledge," in Dieter Henrich (ed.), *Kant oder Hegel* (Stuttgart: Klett-Cotta, 1983), pp. 423–38; p. 426.

[2] Ibid., p. 431.

[3] Richard Rorty, *Philosophy and the Mirror of Nature* (Princeton: Princeton University Press, 1979), p. 178.

[4] Ibid., p. 159.

up the idea that intellectual or political progress is rational, in any sense of 'rational' which is neutral between vocabularies.[5]

[The] notion of a [foundational] "theory of knowledge" will not make sense unless we have confused causation and justification in the manner of Locke.[6]

If we let Ø represent the feature or characteristic, whatever it may be, which distinguishes basic empirical beliefs from other empirical beliefs, then in an acceptable foundationalist account a particular empirical belief B could qualify as basic only if the premises of the following justificatory argument were adequately justified:

(1) B has feature Ø.
(2) Beliefs with feature Ø are highly likely to be true.

Therefore, B is highly likely to be true.

. . . But if all this is correct, we get the disturbing result that B is not basic after all, since its justification depends on that of at least one other empirical belief.[7]

Only a legitimating account of our beliefs about the world will give an understanding of our knowledge of the world. This means that an account of our knowledge of the world must trace it to something that is *ours*, and that is *knowledge*, but that is not *knowledge of the world*.[8]

---

[5] Richard Rorty, *Contingency, Irony, and Solidarity* (Cambridge, UK: Cambridge University Press, 1989), p. 48. Note the ambiguity between "reasons for using languages" that one *has* and adduces, versus reasons that there are whether or not one has them or adduces them. And note also the assumption that only what is based on reasonings from adduced reasons can be assessed as "rational." (One might of course yield the vocabulary of the "rational" in the face of such uninhibited assumptions, for the sake of the conversation, so long as one could still distinguish among beliefs, and even among "choices of vocabulary," those that are "apt," in some apt sense, from those that are not.)

[6] Rorty, *Philosophy and the Mirror of Nature*, p. 152.

[7] Laurence BonJour, *The Structure of Empirical Knowledge* (Cambridge, MA: Harvard Univeristy Press, 1985), p. 31.

[8] Michael Williams, "Epistemological Realism and the Basis of Scepticism," *Mind* NS 97/387 (July 1988), 415–39. (This paper sketches a view developed and

'Formal externalism' shall stand for the denial of formal internalism. And, again, for short we shall drop the qualifier, and speak simply of 'externalism'.

A very wide and powerful current of thinking would sweep away externalism root and branch. This torrent of thought in one way or another encompasses much of contemporary philosophy, both on the Continent and in the Anglophone sphere, as may be seen in the Continental rejection of presence to the mind as well as in the analytic rejection of the given. The Continentals have been led by Heidegger, Gadamer, Habermas, Foucault, and Derrida to a great variety of anti-foundationalisms, ranging from consensualism and hermeneutics to relativism and contextualism. The tide against the given on this side of the Channel is no less powerful and is illustrated by the passages already cited. Their flight from the given and from presence to the mind dooms others to an irresolvable frustration that recognizes the problems but denies the possibility of any satisfactory solution.[9] Many who now object to externalism in such terms offer little by way of support. Barry Stroud and William

defended in his *Unnatural Doubts* (Oxford: Blackwell Publishers, 1992).) Here Williams is attributing a view to Stroud. But in his paper (and in his book) he evidently agrees that if there were a way of attaining a general philosophical understanding of our knowledge of the world, it would have to be in terms of a legitimating account; and the possibility of a substantially externalist account is never seriously considered.

[9] Such overreaction against objective foundations may drive even someone brilliant to unfortunate excesses in the theory and practice of academic and other politics. Compare the writings of Paul Feyerabend. Moreover, the sort of internalism that enforces capitulation to "circularity"-wielding relativists is not confined to the *avant-garde* we have already consulted. For just one example, earlier in the century, in an otherwise most illuminating paper, Alan Gewirth had this to say: "Consequently, it is circular to say that the basic principles of science are themselves cognitive; for it is these principles or norms which determine whether anything else is to be called cognitive. Moreover, these principles are a selection from among other possible principles—possible, that is, in the sense

Alston are exceptional in spelling out the deep reasons why, in their view, externalism will leave us ultimately dissatisfied. They have made as persuasive a case as can be made for the unacceptability in principle of any externalist epistemology, and have done so on a very simple a priori basis grounded in what seem to be demands inherent to the traditional episte-mological project itself. What follows will focus on their case against externalism, but much of it applies *mutatis mutandis* to the reasoning, such as it is, offered by other thinkers as well. Though the issue before us is phrased in the terms of analytic epistemology, it is a wellspring of main currents of thought that reach beyond analysis and epistemology. Yet the issue and its options, rarely faced directly, are very ill-understood.

One thing is already clear. Given our definition of ex-ternalism as simply the denial of internalism, premise A1 is trivially true and amounts to *p or not-p*.

Note further that an acceptable *internalist* epistemological account of all one's knowledge in some domain D would

---

that they are espoused by people who claim to have 'science' or 'knowledge' by methods which are in important respects different from those grounded in inductive and deductive logic. These other methods include those of Christian Science, astrology, phrenology, tribal medicine-men, and many others. Each of these other methods has its own way of defining what is to be meant by 'fact,' 'knowledge,' and so forth. Hence, if any of these latter is to be called 'non-cognitive,' it will be by reference not to *its* norms or principles but to those of *some* other way of viewing 'science' or 'knowledge.' To claim that any of those is 'absolutely' non-cognitive is to ignore the relativity of all claims of cognitiveness to norms or principles which define what is to be meant by 'cognitive.' . . . Hence, strictly speaking, the choice among different conceptions of 'knowledge' or 'science' cannot itself be said to be made by cognitive means." (From A. Gewirth, "Positive 'Ethics' and Normative 'Science'," *The Philosophical Review* 69 (1960); the passage quoted comes from the thirteenth para.) Here again (as against Rorty some footnotes ago), we might well yield the vocabulary of "choices made by cognitive means," so long as we could keep a distinction between choices or commitments that are "apt" and those that are not, where this is not just something "relative" to raw or brute or "arbitrary" commitments.

be, in the following sense, a "legitimating" account of such knowledge.

> *A is a legitimating account of one's knowledge in domain D* Iff D is a domain of one's beliefs that constitute knowledge and are hence justified (and more), and A specifies the sorts of inferences that justify one's beliefs in D, and does so without circularity or endless regress.

But such an account cannot be attained for all one's knowledge:

> *The impossibility of general, legitimating, philosophical understanding of all one's knowledge*: It is impossible to attain a legitimating account of absolutely all one's own knowledge; such an account admits only justification provided by inference or argument and, since it rules out circular or endlessly regressive inferences, such an account must stop with premises that it supposes or "presupposes" that one is justified in accepting, without explaining how one is justified in accepting them in turn.

Accordingly, premise A2 of argument RA seems clearly right. And it all comes down to premise A3. If we are to resist philosophical skepticism we cannot accept that premise. What then are the prospects for a formal externalist epistemology?

II. Formal Externalism: Its Three Choices

The formal externalist has three main choices today, concerning how a belief attains the status of knowledge, how it acquires the sort of epistemic justification (or aptness or warrant or anyhow the positive epistemic status) required if it is to amount to knowledge. These three choices are:

Coherentism. When a belief is epistemically justified, it is so in virtue of its being part of a coherent body of beliefs (or at least one that is sufficiently coherent and appropriately comprehensive).

Foundationalism of the given. When a belief is epistemically justified, it is so in virtue of being either the taking of the given, the mere recording of what is present to the mind of the believer, or else by being inferred appropriately from such foundations.

Reliabilism. When a belief is epistemically justified, it is so in virtue of deriving from an epistemically, truth-conducively reliable process or faculty or intellectual virtue of belief acquisition.

We shall return to the issue of coherentism below. Suffice it to say for now that the most comprehensive coherence accompanied by the truth of what one believes still will not add up to knowledge. The "new evil demon problem" establishes this as follows. Consider the victim of Descartes' evil demon. In fact, suppose we are now such victims. Surely that will not affect whether or not we are *epistemically justified* in believing what we believe. If we are justified as we are, we would be equally justified so long as nothing changed at all within our whole framework of experiences and beliefs. And if by sheer luck one happened to be right in believing that there is a fire nearby, one's being *both* epistemically justified *and* right would still not add up to one's knowing about the fire. So whatever is to be said for coherence, or even for comprehensive coherence, one thing seems clear: none of that will be enough just on its own to explain fully what a true belief needs in order to be a case of knowledge. For one can have plenty of such comprehensive coherence encompassing one's beliefs and even one's beliefs and experiences, without it all amounting to any knowledge.

It would no doubt be replied that coherence might still constitute epistemic justification, even if knowledge requires more than justified true belief. Thanks to Gettier, after all, we already knew *that* to be so.

There is, however, a newer evil demon, who instills a set of beliefs far richer and more coherent than any ever attained by a normal human. Suppose those beliefs to be unaccompanied by any relevant sensory experiences, and suppose them to exclude, at every point in the relevant stretch of one's intellectual life, any indexical demonstrative beliefs about one's surroundings or states of mind. While including plenty of beliefs about *other* subjects' experiences and demonstrative beliefs, they include none about one's *own* experiences or other states of mind, or about one's surroundings.

It is impossible, I submit, to attain epistemic justification, especially for beliefs about one's contingently surrounding world, while deprived, now and in the relevant earlier stretch, of any relevant experiences or introspective or demonstrative beliefs. No amount of coherent richness of content to one's body of beliefs will help, moreover, if these additions do not remedy the lack of experiences and demonstrative beliefs.

What of foundationalism of the given?

Cogito [ergo] sum, exclaimed Descartes, as he at last found a good apple off the tree of knowledge. By that time many other apples had already been judged defective, or at least not clearly enough undefective. Our perceptual beliefs had not qualified, since we could so easily be fooled into believing something false on the basis of sensory experience. For example, one could fall victim to illusion or hallucination, and, more dramatically, to an evil demon or a mad scientist who manipulated one's soul or one's brain directly, thus creating systematically the sorts of experiences normally indicative of a normal environment. None of this will affect the *cogito*, however, since even if one hallucinates, or if one is manipulated by evil demon or mad scientist, one must still exist and one must still be thinking, if one is to be fooled into thinking something incorrectly. Here's a thought that could never be incorrect: the thought that one exists; and here's another: the thought that one is thinking.

Is it this feature of the *cogito* that explains its special assurance? Is it the fact that one cannot believe it without being right, since believing it ensures its truth? Consider the proposition (a) that I am now standing. This proposition is true but only contingently so: I might have been sitting now. In contrast, it is not only true but necessarily true (b) that either I am standing or I am not standing. Is it the necessity of (b) that accounts for its special certainty as compared with (a)? Not entirely. For much is necessary without being certain, and much is certain without being necessary. Thus, in itself the *cogito*, the proposition that I am thinking, is only true and not necessarily true: I might have been unconscious, or even dead, in which case I would not have been thinking. What is not just contingently true, what is necessarily true, is the fact that *if* I am thinking that I think, *then* I am right: no-one can think that they think without being right. Is it *this*, then, that distinguishes the *cogito* and makes it a legitimately known contingent truth, something of which we can properly be assured?

No, a belief can be true, and can even be infallibly, necessarily true, without being anywhere near justified. Take the proposition that there is no largest prime. Since that proposition is necessarily true, we could not possibly go wrong in believing it. Nevertheless, we are not justified in believing it if we are misplacing our trust in someone when we should know better, and have never seen the proof. So the being competent of a belief is not explained simply by its being one that could not possibly be wrong, or one that even the Cartesian demon could not fool one into believing incorrectly. A groundless belief is one that we hold in the absence of supporting reasons or arguments. Some such beliefs far outstrip others: some amount to knowledge of the obvious, while others are no better than superstition or dogma. We are now looking for something that will help explain the difference, and for some explanation of how this distinguishing feature can make such a difference.

A second main source of competent, groundless beliefs, according to the epistemological tradition, is presence to the mind or what is given in sensory and other experience. What is involved in one's aptly believing something about the character of one's present sensory experience? Traditionally it is required that one be reporting simply how it is in one's experience itself. One must be reporting on the intrinsic, qualitative character of some experience.

But here again, as noted in our introduction, a similar problem arises. Suppose one eyes a well-lit surface with a medium-sized white triangle against a black background. In that case, assuming one is normally sighted, one would have a visual experience of a certain distinctive sort, as if one saw a white triangle against a black background. Introspectively, then, one could easily come to know that one was then having experience of that sort: viz, that one was presented with a white triangular image, or the like. What then is the relevant feature of one's introspective belief, what feature makes one's belief apt, makes it indeed a bit of knowledge?

Is it simply that one is just reporting what is directly present to one's mind, what is given in one's experience?

No, something can be thus present to one's mind or given in one's experience without being assuredly present. Take that same situation and change the white image projected on the black surface from a triangle to a dodecagon. And suppose you believe yourself to be presented with a white dodecagon on a black surface, all other conditions remaining as before. Are you then properly assured about the character of your experience so that your introspective belief can then count as apt belief, and indeed as knowledge? What of someone poor at reporting dodecagons in visual experience, who often confuses them with decagons, but who now happens by luck to be right? Such a belief could hardly count as knowledge or even as competent belief.

What Descartes needs in order to explain the special status of the *cogito* is not just that one cannot incorrectly believe that one thinks, but rather that one could not possibly answer incorrectly the question whether one thinks (at least not sincerely and *in foro interno*). And how can one explain this special status enjoyed by that proposition? Descartes' explanation is of course that even a powerful evil demon could not fool one into thinking incorrectly that one thinks. For if the demon gets one to *think* that one thinks—and how else could he fool one into *thinking* incorrectly that one thinks?—then of course inevitably one *does* think and one is bound to be right.

However, that does only half the job. It explains only how one must be right if one thinks that one thinks. It does not explain why it is that one would never think that one does *not* think. Of course Descartes does *claim* that the proposition that one thinks is not only one with regard to which one enjoys infallibility, such that if one accepts it one must be right. He also thinks that it is an *indubitable* proposition. But whereas he has an explanation for the former fact, a very obvious and incontestable explanation, he has none such for the latter: he offers no similarly compelling explanation of why it is that the *cogito* and other similarly simple, clear, distinct propositions are for us indubitable.

What of the doctrine of the given or of presence to the mind? We saw that having a competent belief about the given can't be the mere recording of what is present to the mind, since sometimes what is present to mind is more complex than what we are *reliably* able to record. We can, however, improve on the doctrine of the given in keeping with our insights from Descartes. Here the proposal would be that one aptly introspects P iff P describes a present state of one's own consciousness and while considering attentively and with a clear mind the question whether P is the case, one believes P; and it is very unlikely that one would ever opt wrong on such a proposition when in such circumstances.[10]

By reflecting on how the doctrine of the given needs to be formulated if it is to meet certain objections, we have arrived at a virtue-theoretic version of foundationalism. What matters is not that one be attending to the contents of one's mind, to the experiences or beliefs or other states of mind that one may be in, nor is what matters that one be attending to simple necessary truths. For simplicity is a relative matter, and what is simple for an experienced mathematician is far from it for the schoolchild learning arithmetic. What matters is rather that the object of knowledge be something about which the subject is a reliable judge, one very unlikely to

---

[10] This is discussed more fully in L. BonJour and E. Sosa, *Epistemic Justification* (Oxford: Blackwell Publishers, 2003).

opt wrong. And it matters further that in hitting the mark of truth one manifest such a competence.

So we are down to the third and last of the options open to the formal externalist. But I view generic reliabilism as a *very* broad category indeed, one capacious enough to include thinkers as diverse as René Descartes and Alvin Goldman. If we are to resist philosophical skepticism it would appear that here we must make a stand. For, remember, if A3 cannot be defeated, then philosophical skepticism is the inevitable consequence. So let us consider some of the objections that have been pressed against generic reliabilism. Here we turn to the promised arguments by Stroud and Alston, and also to some reasoning due to Paul Moser.

III. Objections to Reliabilism and Externalism

According to Stroud " . . . we need some reason to accept a theory of knowledge if we are going to rely on that theory to understand how our knowledge is possible. That is what . . . no form of 'externalism' can give a satisfactory account of."[11] Against Descartes, for example, and against the "externalist" in general he objects on the basis of the following *meta-epistemic requirement*:

> MR In order to understand one's knowledge satisfactorily one must see oneself as having some reason to accept a theory that one can recognize would explain one's knowledge if it were true.

[11] Barry Stroud, "Understanding Human Knowledge in General," in Marjorie Clay and Keith Lehrer (eds.), *Knowledge and Skepticism* (Boulder: Westview, 1989), p. 43.

And how is MR to be defended? From the assumptions: (a) that understanding something requires having good reason for accepting a potential explanation, something that would be an explanation if it were true, and (b) that, as a generality-thirsty theorist of knowledge, one wants to understand how one knows the things one thinks one knows.[12] But MR does not follow from these assumptions. From these assumptions it follows only that in order to understand one's knowledge one must *have* a good enough reason, and must accept some appropriate explanation on that rational basis. Why must one also *see oneself as having* such reason?

Far from being just an isolated slip, MR represents rather a deeply held intuition that underlies a certain way of thinking about epistemology. We have seen already several passages that fit this intuition. According to such internalism, what is important in epistemology is justification; and the justi-fication of any given belief requires appeal to *other* beliefs that constitute one's reasons for holding the given belief. Of course, when one combines this with rejection of circularity, as Stroud does, the case for skepticism is very strong, assum-ing that for limited humans an infinite regress of reasons or justifications is out of the question.

The externalist therefore wants to allow some *other* way for a belief to acquire the epistemic status required for it to be knowledge, some way *other* than the belief's being

---

[12] Compare ibid., p. 44: "[Descartes is] . . . a theorist of knowledge. He wants to understand how he knows the things he thinks he knows. And he cannot satisfy himself on that score unless he can see himself as having some reason to accept the theory that he (and all the rest of us) can recognize would explain his knowledge if it were true. That is not because knowing implies knowing that you know. It is because having an explanation of something in the sense of understanding it is a matter of having good reason to accept something that would be an explanation if it were true."

based on some justification, argument, or reason. Note, moreover, how very broad this sense of "externalism" is. Even arch-internalist Descartes is an "externalist" in our present sense. So we distinguish our present externalism as "*formal* externalism," which brings with it a corresponding type of internalism, "formal internalism." Formal internalism holds that there is only one way a belief can have the positive epistemic status required for it to be knowledge, and that way is the belief's having the backing of reasons or arguments. Note the connection with the requirement that a philosophically satisfactory account of how one knows must be a *legitimating* account, one that specifies the reasons favoring one's belief. Obviously, a formal internalist will believe that for *every* belief that amounts to knowledge there must be such a legitimating account, and that only once we have such an account can we understand what makes that belief knowledge.

Consider now the naturalist, externalist epistemologist. He will understand how people know the things they do, only if he knows or has some reason to believe his scientific account of the world around him. According to Stroud, this dooms our epistemologist:

If his goal was, among other things, to explain our scientific knowledge of the world around us, he will have an explanation of such knowledge only if he can see himself as possessing some knowledge in that domain. In studying other people, that presents no difficulty. It is precisely by knowing what he does about the world that he explains how others know what they do about the world. But if he had started out asking how anyone knows anything at all about the world, he would be no further along towards understanding how any of it is possible if he had not understood how he himself knows what he has to know about the world in order to have any explanation at all. He must understand himself as knowing or having some reason to believe that his theory is true.[13]

But it is again unclear why the epistemologist needs to see himself as having justification for his theory, or as knowing his theory, in order for it to give him understanding of how he and others know the things they know, either in general or in the domain in question. Why is it not enough that he in fact *have good reason to accept his theory* or perhaps even *know his theory to be true*? This is different from his knowing that he has good reason to believe his epistemologically explanatory theory, or even knowing that he knows his theory to be true. To this the response is as follows.

[The externalist epistemologist] . . . is at best in the position of someone who has good reason to believe his theory if that theory is in fact true, but has no such reason to believe it if some other theory is true instead. He can see what he *would* have good reason to believe if the theory he believes were true, but he cannot see or understand himself as knowing or having good reason to believe what his theory says.[14]

[Even]. . . if it is true that you can know something without knowing that you know it, the philosophical theorist of knowledge cannot simply insist on the point and expect to find acceptance of an "externalist" account of knowledge fully satisfactory. If he could, he would be in the position of someone who says: "I don't know whether I understand human knowledge or not. If what I believe about it is true and my beliefs about it are produced in what my theory says is the right way, I do know how human knowledge comes to be, so in that sense I do understand. But if my beliefs are not true, or not arrived at in that way, I do not. I wonder which it is. I wonder whether I understand human knowledge or

---

[13] Stroud, "Understanding Human Knowledge in General," p. 45.
[14] Ibid., p. 46.

not." That is not a satisfactory position to arrive at in one's study of human knowledge—or of anything else.[15]

But again it is hard to see why the externalist theorist of knowledge must be in that position. Suppose that, as suggested earlier, he does *not* have to say or believe that he *does* know his theory of knowledge. Suppose he does not after all need to satisfy MR. Must he then say or believe that he *does not* know his theory of knowledge? Must he begin to wonder *whether* his theory of knowledge is true, or whether he does really understand human knowledge or not? Surely not.

Here the dialectic is given a further twist. It is replied that the sort of understanding of our knowledge of the external that we want in philosophy is not just understanding by dumb luck. What we want is rather *knowledgeable* understanding. And this we will never have until we are in a good position to accept our view of our own faculties (of perception or memory, for example), a view that properly underlies our trust in their reliability. But this view we will never be able to justify without relying in turn on already attained knowledge of the external. And this precludes our ever attaining a philosophically satisfactory understanding of all our knowledge in that domain.[16]

---

[15] Stroud, "Understanding Human Knowledge in General," p. 47.

[16] Compare Stroud on this: "We want witting, not unwitting, understanding. That requires knowing or having some reason to accept the scientific story you believe about how people know the things they know. And in the case of knowledge of the world around us, that would involve already knowing or having some reason to believe something in the domain in question. Not all the knowledge in that domain would thereby be explained." (Ibid., p. 48.) Also: "The demand for completely general understanding of knowledge in a certain domain requires that we see ourselves at the outset as not knowing anything in that domain and then coming to have such knowledge on the basis of some independent and in that sense prior knowledge or experience. . . . [When] we try to explain how we know . . . things [in a domain we are interested in] we

Of course, the dialectic of the *diallelus* is about as ancient as philosophy itself. Nor is Stroud the *only* philosopher today who argues against formal externalism. William Alston, for example, has discussed these issues extensively, featuring the following main theme:

> . . . *if sense-perception is reliable*, a track-record argument will suffice to show that it is. Epistemic circularity does not in and of itself disqualify the argument. But even granting that point, the argument will not do its job unless we *are* justified in accepting its premises; and that is the case only if sense perception is in fact reliable. And this is to offer a stone instead of bread. We can say the same of any belief-forming practice whatever, no matter how disreputable. We can just as well say of crystal-ball gazing that if it *is* reliable, we can use a track record argument to show that it is reliable. But when we ask whether one or another source of belief is reliable, we are interested in *discriminating* those that can reasonably be trusted from those that cannot. Hence merely showing that *if* a given source is reliable it can be shown by its record to be reliable, does nothing to indicate that the source belongs with the sheep rather than with the goats. I have removed an allegedly crippling disability, but I have not given the argument a clean bill of health.[17]

find we can understand it only by assuming that we have got some knowledge in the domain in question. And that is not philosophically satisfying. We have lost the prospect of explaining and therefore understanding all of our knowledge with complete generality." (Ibid., pp. 48–9.)

[17] W. P. Alston, *Perceiving God: The Epistemology of Religious Experience* (Ithaca: Cornell University Press, 1991), p. 148. In a review of my *Knowledge in Perspective* in *Mind*, NS 102/405 (Jan. 1993), 199–203. Alston adds that ". . . it is plausible to suppose that we cannot give an impressive argument for the reliability of sense perception without making use of what we have learned from sense perception. This problem affects Sosa's view as much as it does any other form of externalism that requires for justification or knowledge that the source of a belief be truth-conducive. To apply Sosa's view we would have to determine which belief forming habits are intellectual virtues, i.e., which can be depended on to yield mostly true beliefs. Doesn't epistemic circularity attach to these enterprises, by his own showing? What does he have to say about that?"

And compare Paul Moser's statement of the difficulty as he sees it:

What . . . can effectively justify one's meta-belief in the virtue of memory? What can effectively justify the claim that "the products of such faculties are likely to be true"? These questions . . . ask what, if anything, can provide a cogent defense of the alleged reliability of memory against familiar skeptical queries. . . . The . . . questions ask not for absolute proof, but for a non-question-begging reason supporting the alleged reliability of memory, a reason that does not beg a key question against the skeptic. It is doubtful that we can deliver such a reason; coherence of mere beliefs will surely not do the job.[18]

Such reasoning by Stroud, Alston, and Moser (and many others along the historical length and contemporary breadth of philosophy) may just return us to the questionable assumption that a satisfyingly general philosophical account of human knowledge would have to be a legitimating account that would reveal how all such knowledge can be traced back to some epistemically prior knowledge and shown to be inferentially derivable from such prior knowledge. There is no good reason to make this assumption, especially when it is so easy to see that no such general account of all our knowledge could conceivably be obtained.

[18] Paul Moser, Review of *Knowledge in Perspective*, in *Canadian Philosophical Reviews* 11 (1991): 425–7. T. E. Wilkerson also joins a broad consensus against the supposed "circularity" in externalism: "How can I know that I am intellectually virtuous, that I have a settled ability or disposition to arrive at the truth? Indeed, how do I know that I have arrived at the truth? As Sosa points out, it is no good to answer that my beliefs are true in so far as they are justified by other beliefs: that way lies *either* old-fashioned foundationalism *or* coherentism. Nor presumably is it any good to say that they are justified because they have been acquired in an intellectually virtuous way: the circle seems swift and unbreakable." (Review of *Knowledge in Perspective*, in *Philosophical Books* 33 (1992): 159–61.) This near-consensus remains to the present day, though a forthcoming book by Michael Bergmann joins in opposing it.

IV. Legitimation and Explanation in Philosophical Accounts of Knowledge

The desire for a fully general, legitimating, philosophical understanding of all our knowledge is unfulfillable. It is unfulfillable for simple, demonstrable logical reasons. In this respect it is like the desire to find the patron saint of modesty: he who blesses all and only those who do not bless themselves. A trek through the Himalayas may turn up likely prospects each of whom eventually is seen to fall short, until someone in the expedition reflects that there could not possibly be such a saint, and this for evident, logical reasons. How should they all respond to this result? They may of course be very unhappy to have been taken in by a project now clearly shown to be inherently defective, and this may leave them frustrated and dissatisfied. But is it reasonable for them to insist that somehow the objective is still worthy, even if unfortunately it turns out to be incoherent? Is this a sensible response? How would we respond if we found ourselves in that situation? Would it not be a requirement of good sense or even of sanity to put that obviously incoherent project behind us, to just forget about it and to put our time to better use? And is that not what we must do with regard to the search for fully general, legitimating, philosophical accounts of our knowledge?

If it does not just return us to that questionable assumption, however, then what can be the basis for the objection to a general theory of knowledge, indeed to one so general that it encompasses not only all our knowledge of the external but all our knowledge in general. Suppose one's theory takes the following form:

T A belief X amounts to knowledge if and only if it satisfies conditions C.

It would not be long before a philosopher would wonder what makes belief in T itself a piece of knowledge, and if T is held as an explanatory theory for all of our knowledge, then the answer would not be far to seek: belief of T amounts to knowledge because belief of T itself meets conditions C. And how do we know that belief of T meets conditions C? Well, of course, *that* belief itself must meet conditions C in turn. And so on, without end. Is there any unacceptability in principle here, is there any unavoidable viciousness?

Compare the following three things.

E A belief B in a general epistemological account of when beliefs are justified (or competent) that applies to B itself and explains in virtue of what it, too, is justified.

G A statement S of a general account of when statements are grammatical (or a sentence S stating when sentences are grammatical) that applies to S itself and explains in virtue of what it, too, is grammatical.

P A belief B in a general psychological account of why one acquires and retains the beliefs one holds, an account that applies to B itself and explains why it, too, is held.

Why should E be any more problematic than G or P? Why should there be any more of a problem for a general epistemology than there would be for a general grammar the grammaticality of whose statement is explained in turn by itself, or for a general psychology belief in which is explained by that very psychology?

It must be granted that what we want is a sort of explanation that would in principle enable us to understand how we have any knowledge at all. Question: "Why are there chickens?"

Answer: "They come from eggs." "And why are there eggs?" "They come from chickens." This exchange could not provide a complete answer to a child's question, if the question is, more fully, that of why there are chickens *at all, ever*. To answer this question we need appeal to divine creation, or evolution, or anyhow to something entirely other than chickens. Consider now the analogous question about knowledge, about the sources of the epistemic status of our knowledgeable beliefs (and not now about the causal sources of their existence). A complete answer for this question must appeal to something other than beliefs that already enjoy the status of knowledge. For we want an explanation of how beliefs *ever* attain that status *at all*.

It is important to avert a confusion. We shall never be able really to *have* an explanation of anything without our *having* some knowledge, the knowledge that constitutes our having the explanation, knowledge like

K X is the case in virtue of such and such.

Though we must have such knowledge if we are to understand why X is the case, however, there is no need to include any attribution of knowledge in the explanans of K, in the "such and such." The concept of knowledge need not be part of that explanans. Compare again our general theory of knowledge schema:

T A belief X amounts to knowledge if and only if it satisfies conditions C.

T is something we must *know* if it is to give us real understanding, and in offering it we are in some sense "presupposing" that we know it. This does not mean that our theory must be less than fully general. Our theory T may still be fully general so long as no epistemic status—e.g., knowledge, or justification—plays any role in the "conditions C" that constitute the explanans of T.

It is true that in epistemology we want *knowledgeable* understanding, and not just "understanding by dumb luck" (which, in the relevant sense, is incoherent anyhow, and hence not to be had; to understand why is to know why, and knowledge is incompatible with getting it right by dumb luck). But there is no apparent reason why we cannot have it with a theory such as T, without compromising the full generality of our account. Of course in explaining how we know theory T, whether to the skeptic or to ourselves, we have to appeal to theory T itself, given the assumptions of correctness and full generality that we are making concerning T. Given those assumptions, there seems no way of correctly answering such a skeptic except by "begging the question" and "arguing circularly" against him. But, once we understand this, what option is left to us except to go ahead and "beg" that question against *such* a skeptic (though "begging the question" may now be a misnomer for what we do, since it is surely no fallacy, not if it constitutes correct and legitimate intellectual procedure). Nor are we, in proceeding thus, by means of a self-supporting argument, assuming that *all self-supporting arguments are on a par*. This would be a serious mistake. It is not just *in virtue of being self-supporting* that our belief in T would acquire its epistemic status required for knowledge. Rather it would be in virtue of meeting conditions C. And conditions C must not yield that a belief or a system of beliefs has the appropriate positive epistemic status provided simply that it is self-supporting. For this would obviously be inadequate. Therefore, our belief in T *would* be self-supporting, as had better be any successful and general theory of knowledge, but it would not amount to knowledge or even to a belief with the appropriate epistemic status, *simply in virtue of being self-supporting.*

V. Conclusion

In all our reflection and in all our discussion of objections to externalism we have found no good reason to yield to the skeptic or to reject externalist theories of knowledge globally and antecedently as theories that could not possibly give us the kind of understanding of human knowledge in general that is a goal of epistemology. And so we have found no good reason to accept *philosophical skepticism*, the main target thesis of this chapter.

The philosophical skeptic has not made his case, then, and it remains possible for us to understand our epistemic sources, while still retaining the knowledge that we ordinarily take ourselves to have, and while we still understand its sources in quite general terms. But it remains to be seen how more specifically to defend our claim to have such knowledge, and how to explain its sources. We next reconsider a notorious attempt. We return to Moore's so-called proof of the external world. We reconsider, from another angle, its relation to our Cartesian key to the resolution of fundamental problems of epistemology.

Chapter 9

Reflective Knowledge
in the Best Circles

I. Indirect Realism Redux

Familiar skeptical scenarios—dreaming, evil demon, brain in a vat, etc.—show that our experience prompts but does not logically entail its corresponding perceptual beliefs. Experience as if there is a fire before us does not entail that there is a fire there, experience as if here is a hand does not entail that here is a hand, etc. *Perhaps* what is required for one's beliefs and experiences to have certain contents entails that these could not possibly be *entirely* false or misleading. Indeed, some such conclusion follows from certain externalist and epistemic requirements on one's justified attribution of familiar contents to one's own experiences or beliefs. But even if that much *is* right—which is still controversial—one's experience or belief that here is a hand, or yonder a fire, might still be wildly off the mark. We cannot deduce much of our supposed knowledge of the external from unaided premises about our experience.

As for inductive or analogical reasoning, only abductive reasoning—inference to the best explanation—offers much promise, but it seems questionable as a solution to our problem.[1] Suppose (a) that we restrict ourselves to data just about the qualitative character of our own sensory experience, and (b) that we view belief in a commonsensical external world as a theory postulated to explain the course of our experience. What exactly is the proposal? Is it proposed that when ordinarily we accept the presence of a hand before us, we *do* know, and know on the basis of an abductive inference; or is it proposed rather that in such circumstances we have resources that *would* enable us to know if only we used those resources to make effective abductive arguments? The second, more modest, proposal is *too* modest, since it leaves our ordinary perceptual beliefs in a position like that of a theorem accepted through a guess or a blunder, one that we do have the resources to prove after much hard thought, but one that we have not come close to proving at the time when we are just guessing or blundering.

Even the modest proposal, moreover, seems unlikely to succeed. *Could* we form a rich enough set of beliefs purely about the qualitative character of our sensory experience, one rich enough to permit abductive inferences yielding our commonsense view of external reality? This seems doubtful when we consider (a) that such pure data beliefs could not already presuppose the external reality to be inferred, and (b) that the postulated commonsense "theory" of external reality must presumably meet constraints on abductive

---

[1] For Russell the "common sense hypothesis" of independent physical objects is "simpler" than the supposition that life is but a dream (as he explains in chapter II of *The Problems of Philosophy* (1912; New York: Oxford Univeristy Press, 1997), pp. vii–xxvi). For Quine the "hypothesis of ordinary physical objects" is "posited" or "projected" from the data provided by sensory stimulations. "Subtracting his cues from his world view, we get man's net contribution as the difference." (*Word and Object* (Cambridge, Mass: MIT Press, 1960), p. 5.) That Quine's position is deeply problematic is shown by Stroud (*The Significance of Philosophical Scepticism* (Oxford: Oxford University Press, 1984), ch. VI).

inference: e.g., that the postulated theory be empirically testable and also simpler and less *ad hoc* than alternatives (e.g., Berkeley's). These requirements plausibly imply that our data must go beyond detached observations, and include some acceptable correlations. Yet these correlations are unavailable if we restrict ourselves to beliefs about the character of our experience.[2] Most especially are they unavailable, and most especially is the postulated inference implausible, when our database is restricted, as it is by G. E. Moore, to introspectively known facts of one's own *then present* subjective experience, and to *directly recalled* facts of one's own earlier experience. (If deprived of the epistemic resources of testimony and of retentive memory—except insofar as such resources can be validated by reason-cum-introspection, which is not very far if at all—then there is precious little we can any longer see ourselves as knowing, thus deprived.)

Accordingly, the skeptic has a powerful case against Moore's claim that our knowledge of the external is based on an inductive or analogical inference from such information about our experience.[3] It is not realistic to suppose that we consciously make such inferences in everyday life. It is less implausible to conceive of such inferences as implicit and/or dispositional, but even this strains belief. Besides, even granted that we make such inferences if only implicitly, do they yield simpler and less *ad hoc* hypotheses than alternatives? That is far from clear; nor do such hypotheses seem empirically testable and credible simply as explanations of the purely qualitative character of our then present or directly recalled experience.

---

[2] This is argued by Wilfrid Sellars in "Phenomenalism," in his *Science, Perception, and Reality* (London: Routledge and Kegan Paul, 1963).

[3] A claim examined in Chapter 1 above.

Having reached a dead end, let us have some second thoughts on Moore's view of perceptual beliefs as inferential. Here he joined a venerable tradition along with Russell himself. If perceptual knowledge is thus mediate and inferential, what knowledge can qualify as immediate and foundational? Modern philosophy begins with Descartes' canonical answer to this question.[4]

II. Descartes' Circles

Descartes had two circles, not only the big famous one involving God as guarantor of our faculties, but also a smaller one found in the second paragraph of his Third Meditation, where he reasons like this:

I am certain that I am a thinking being. Do I not therefore also know what is required for my being certain about anything? In this first item of knowledge there is simply a clear and distinct perception of what I am asserting; this would not be enough to make me certain of the truth of the matter if it could ever turn out that something which I perceived with such clarity and distinctness was false. So I now seem to be able to lay it down as a general rule that whatever I perceive very clearly and distinctly is true.[5]

And yet when he looks away from particular clear and distinct items such as the proposition that he is a thinking

---

[4] The shift to discussion of Descartes may seem abrupt; however, what we find about the nature of immediate knowledge in that discussion has important implications for a position that Moore failed to explore. Skeptics who are willing to grant Descartes his immediate knowledge through introspection or rational intuition would need to explain exactly why perception could never yield such knowledge. (And what of memory?) The discussion of Descartes to follow is meant to highlight this issue.

[5] *The Philosophical Writings of Descartes*, ed. J. Cottingham, R. Stoothoff, and D. Murdoch (Cambridge: Cambridge University Press, 1975), Vol. II, p. 24.

being, Descartes grants that a powerful enough being could deceive him even about what seems most manifest. Descartes grants that he could be astray in his beliefs as to what he perceives or remembers, and even in taking himself to intuit something clearly and distinctly. This doubt must be blocked if one is to attain certainty by intuiting something clearly and distinctly. Accordingly, Descartes launches the theological reflections that lead eventually to his non-deceiving God.

Even without the further boost of certainty provided by the proof of a non-deceiving God, however, Descartes takes himself to have attained some positive justification. Early in the Third Meditation he takes himself to perceive clearly and distinctly that he is a thinking being, which he takes to be what gives him the certainty that he is indeed such a being. And he reasons that this clear and distinct perception would *not* give him such certainty if it were less than perfectly reliable, and apparently *concludes from this* that his clear and distinct perception *is* perfectly reliable. One could demand how he knows all these things: how he can be sure that he does clearly and distinctly perceive that he thinks, for one thing; and how he can be sure that there is nothing else in his situation that could provide the degree of certainty involved; and how he can be sure that the clarity and distinctness of his perception could not possibly provide that degree of certainty unless it were infallible. What could he say in response? Descartes might well have a uniform response to all such questions: in each case he might appeal once again to clear and distinct perception, each of the things in question being something we are assured of by our clearly and distinctly perceiving *it*.

About his belief that he is a thinking being, I wish to highlight, not Descartes' answers to such questions, however, but the inference that he draws: *So I now seem to be able to lay it down as a general rule that whatever I perceive very clearly and distinctly is true.* Just what is Descartes' argument in support of this general rule? Might his reasoning take the following form, for example, if it sets out from the *cogito*?

1. Datum: I know with a high degree of certainty that I think.
2. I clearly and distinctly perceive that I think, and that is the only, or anyhow the best account of the source of my knowledge that I think.
3. So my clear and distinct perception that I think is what explains why or how it is that I know I think.
4. But my clear and distinct perception could not serve as a source of that knowledge if it were not an infallibly reliable faculty.
5. So, finally, my clear and distinct perception must be an infallibly reliable faculty.

The move from 1 and 2 to 3 is an inference to an explanatory account that one might accept for the coherence it gives to one's view of things in the domain involved. Descartes does elsewhere appeal to coherence at important junctures.[6] So he may be doing so here as well, although questions do arise about how Descartes views coherence. Does he accept the power of coherence to add justified certainty, and, in particular, would he claim infallibility for

---

[6] In his *Principles of Philosophy* (Part IV, art. 205) for example, he notes that if we can interpret a long stretch of otherwise undecipherable writing by supposing that it is written in "one-off natural language," where the alphabet has all been switched forward by one letter, etc., then this is good reason for that interpretation. There he also argues for his scientific account of reality in terms of certain principles by claiming that " . . . it would hardly have been possible for so many items to fall into a coherent pattern if the original principles had been false." (From p. 290 of J. Cottingham, R. Stoothoff, and D. Murdock, op. cit.)

(sufficiently comprehensive and binding) coherence as he does for clear and distinct intuition?[7] In any case, the comprehensive coherence of his worldview *would* be enhanced by an explanation of how clear and distinct perception comes to be so highly reliable, even infallible. And this is just what Descartes attempts, through his theological and other reasoning. Descartes can see that reason might take him to a position that is sufficiently comprehensive and interlocking—and thereby defensible against any foreseeable attack, no holds barred, against any specific doubt actually pressed or in the offing, no matter how slight. Unaided reason might take him to that position. Need he go any further? What is more: Might one reach a similar position while dispensing with the trappings of Cartesian rationalism?

III. Circular Externalism

Compare now how Moore might have proceeded:

1. Datum: I know with a high degree of certainty that here is a hand.

2. I can see and feel that here is a hand, and that is the only, or anyhow the best account of the source of my knowledge that here is a hand.

3. So my perception that here is a hand is what explains why or how it is that I know (with certainty) that here is a hand.

[7] My attribution to Descartes is tentative because of the enormous bibliography on the "Cartesian Circle." In deference to that important tradition of scholarship, I do no more than *suggest* that there is logical space for an interpretation of Descartes more complex than many already tried, but coherent and interesting nonetheless. (I am myself convinced that this *is* Descartes' actual position, and defend this more fully below.)

4. But my perception could not serve as a source of that degree of justified certainty if it were not a reliable faculty.[8]

5. So, finally, my perception must be a reliable faculty.

Moore could of course go on to say more about the nature of the perception that assures him about the hand. He might still say that such perception involves an implicit inference from what is known immediately and introspectively, perhaps an inductive or analogical inference of some sort. And that might make his view more comprehensively coherent, but we have already seen reasons why postulating such an inference is questionable. So we focus rather on a second alternative: Moore might well take perceiving to involve no inference at all, not even implicit inference, but only transfer of light, nerve impulses, etc., in such a way that the character of one's surroundings has a distinctive impact on oneself and occasions corresponding and reliable beliefs. This might also amount eventually to a comprehensively coherent view of one's knowledge of the external world. *And its epistemologically significant features would not distinguish it in any fundamental respect from the procedure followed by Descartes.*

The theme of accidentally true belief has loomed large in the epistemology of recent decades. The Gettier problem, for example, is posed by a justified belief true for reasons far removed from whatever causes it to be held and justified. Externalist conceptions of propositional knowledge focus on this theme: take, e.g., one offered by Peter Unger (non-accidentally true belief) and one offered by Alvin Goldman (belief caused by the truth of its content). And Nozick's tracking account is also a conception of this sort: S knows

---

[8] Here one would reduce Descartes' requirement of *infallible* certainty.

that p if and only if S believes correctly that p, and also (in the circumstances): *both* it would have been true that p only if S had believed it, *and* if it had not been true that p, then S would not have believed it.

Why are these conceptions of knowledge of special interest to us here? Because each offers a way to explain how one can know that p without reasoning from prior knowledge. The key idea exploited is this: you can know something non-inferentially so long as it is no accident or coincidence that you are right.

Both the tracking and the causal accounts defensibly require a special non-accidental connection between the belief and the fact believed. Nevertheless, in each case other levels of accidentality remain. Suppose I fancy myself a connossieur of tomato ripeness, but suffer from a rare form of color blindness that precludes my discerning nearly any shade of red except that displayed by this particular tomato. Therefore my judgments of tomato ripeness are in general apt to be right with no better than even chance. But when it's the particular (and rare) shade of red now displayed, then I am nearly infallible. Oblivious to my affliction, however, I issue judgments of tomato ripeness with abandon over a wide spectrum of shades of red. Assuming that, unknown to me, the variety of tomato involved always ripens with this shade of red, then my belief that this tomato is ripe *is* in step with the truth, and arguably satisfies the requirements of Unger, Goldman, and Nozick. But, again, it is nevertheless in some relevant sense or respect only an accident that I am right in my belief.[9] We need a clearer and more comprehensive view

---

[9] For an early statement of this sort of problem, urged against Nozickian tracking, see Colin McGinn's "The Concept of Knowledge," *Midwest Studies in Philosophy* 9 (1984): 529–54.

of the respects in which one's belief must be non-accidentally true if it is to constitute knowledge.

Unaided, the tracking or causal requirements proposed suffer from a sort of tunnel vision. They permit too narrow a focus on the particular target belief and its causal or counterfactual relation to the truth of its content. Just widening our focus will not do, however, if we widen it only far enough to include the process that yields the belief involved. We need an even broader view.

IV. Virtue Epistemology

[When] . . . thought is concerned with study, not with action or production, its good or bad state consists [simply] in being true or false. For truth is the function of whatever thinks. . . .[10]

Hence the function of each of the understanding parts is truth; and so the virtue of each part will be the state that makes that part grasp the truth most of all.[11]

Virtue epistemology is distinguished by its emphasis on the *subject* as seat of justification. In order to qualify as knowledge a belief must be "competent," epistemically so, in a strong sense that goes beyond its being just a belief that coheres well within the subject's perspective. The "tracking account" (Nozick) sees here little more than a claim about that belief's counterfactual relation to the truth of what is believed. "Reliable indicator" accounts require rather that the belief itself or the reasons for it have properties nomically sufficient for its truth (Armstrong, Swain). "Reliable process" accounts focus instead on the cognitive process that yields the belief,

---

[10] Aristotle, *Nicomachean Ethics*, 1139a27–30; trans. T. Irwin.
[11] Ibid., 1139b11–13.

and on the truth ratio in the products of that process, actual and counterfactual (Alvin Goldman).

It is rather the subject and her cognitive virtues or aptitudes that hold primary interest for virtue epistemology. Consider the athletic virtues of a tennis champion. When we say that a shot is not just a winning shot but a skillful one, we imply a comment on the player as shotmaker. Suppose a tyro wields a racquet on a court and, unaware of the approaching ball, issues what amounts by luck to a stylish and effective backhand winner. Such a shot might be an unreturnable winning shot, but it would manifest no real skill.

Why are we unwilling to admire a performance as "skillful" if it manifests only a fleeting, or even an instantaneous state of the agent's? Skills, abilities, competences, aptitudes, prowess—these come and go, true enough, but they do not flit by instantaneously. Why not? Why do we tend to define these concepts so as to require such stability? We might have defined similar concepts without requiring stability. Why do we define these concepts as we do? Why have we adopted these and not others? Should one not expect that, other things being equal, the more clearly useful a concept is to us, the more likely it is that we shall retain it? People need to know who are dependable members of their group—this is a *kind* of thing we need to monitor in a great variety of contexts, with a great variety of objectives. Cooperative success depends on the group's ability to monitor people's aptitudes and ineptitudes. So it is no surprise that the sorts of aptitudes (skills, competences, virtues) that we recognize and admire are those that linger stably.[12]

---

[12] The social utility of concepts is invoked occasionally to defend a proposed account of knowledge in my *Knowledge in Perspective* (Cambridge: Cambridge University Press, 1991); e.g., on pp. 27 and 275. The form of argument involved

To praise a performance as skillful or an action as right, or a judgment as wise or apt, accordingly, is to assess not only the action or the judgment, but also the reflected aptitude or character or intelligence. This is a distinctive view with versions both in epistemology and in ethics. It is distinctive in that the rightness of an action (or a choice) and the aptness (or positive epistemic status) of a belief would involve not just whether the performance is *optimific* (if an action) or *true* (if a belief); nor just whether a good enough procedure was followed, *perhaps accidentally*, in arriving at that choice, or whether a good enough cognitive process chanced to lead to the belief; nor even just whether a rule somehow in effect demands that choice or that belief in those circumstances. Our virtue epistemology and virtue ethics focus rather on the agent and cognizer. When the agent's actions are said to be *right* and the cognizer's beliefs *knowledge*, we speak implicitly of the virtues, practical or intellectual, seated in that subject, which (a) give rise to that action or belief, adding to the subject's worth as agent or cognizer, and which (b) make him reliable and trustworthy over an interesting spread of possible choices or beliefs, and circumstances.

V. Virtue and Coherence

Can we explain what distinguishes a system of beliefs (and experiences) that, internally regarded, is intellectually virtuous and admirable? Presumably our explanation would involve the system's explanatory coherence, its overall simplicity and lack of *ad hoc* epicycles, and so on. Philosophical mythology

is used insightfully in E. J. Craig's *Knowledge and the State of Nature* (Oxford: Clarendon Press, 1990), where it takes center stage.

contains creatures who excel in all such respects, however, though their beliefs fall short of being knowledge even when true. Take the brain in a vat, for example, or the victim of the evil demon. An adult recently envatted, or victimized by the demon, can be indistinguishable from the best of us in respect of the comprehensiveness and coherence of their beliefs and experiences. Even when right about environing objects and events, such a victim's beliefs are far from being knowledge.

Might such comprehensive internal coherence exhaust all cognitive or intellectual competence, at least when it comprises not only beliefs but also experiences? Not if it is part of competence to get it right non-accidentally. For such mental coherence might conceivably be detached from the environing world of the thinker, so as to deprive him of reliable access to the truth. And this would leave him short of a kind of cognitive or intellectual competence, that which consists at least in part in being so constituted and so situated as to enjoy such reliable access. Someone who is sufficiently drunk or in the dark is thereby deprived of a kind of perceptual competence, even if his plight is only temporary, and even if at a deeper level he is gifted with excellent visual competence. Of course, even if it cannot exhaust cognitive or intellectual competence, coherence is valued not only by philosophers but by the reflective more generally. But one also wants faculties and virtues beyond reflective, coherence-seeking reason: perception, for example, and memory. Equally, internal coherence goes beyond such faculties, and requires reason, which counts for a lot in its own right. But why should that be so, if comprehensive coherence is no guarantee of truth, if the internal coherence enjoyed by the envatted yields little if any truth?

Compare first reason with memory. Input beliefs are required for retentive memory and inferential reason, which then yield beliefs as outputs. Retentive memory yields again the input belief itself, while inferential reason yields a new belief. Even the most excellent transmission faculty will not guarantee the truth of its output, which will depend not only on the transmission but also on the inputs. But our transmission faculties are valuable even so, if only because they *combine* with other faculties to increase vastly the total yield of true beliefs.

How does internal coherence, of little significant epistemic value in itself, become more valuable when combined with external competence? Coherence-seeking inferential reason, like retentive memory, is valuable when combined with externally competent faculties of perception, because when so combined it, like retentive memory, gives us a more comprehensive grasp of the truth than we would have in its absence.

Good perception is in part constituted by certain transitions from experiences to corresponding beliefs—as is the transition from the visual experience characteristic of a tomato seen in good light to belief in the tomato. Other such transitions help constitute good introspection, as when one's headache prompts awareness of it as a headache. Finally, if the comprehensive coherence of one's system of beliefs is at least in part responsible for its constitution and persistence, it thereby manifests a rational competence. Such comprehensive coherence is not just mechanical, but must reflect appropriate sensitivity to adhocness, simplicity, and explanatory power. And it must include, not only belief/belief connections, but also experience/belief connections constitutive of good perception, and conscious-state/belief connections constitutive of good introspection. This broader conception of the coherence of one's mind involves not only the logical, probabilistic, and explanatory relations among one's first-order beliefs, but also coherence between these beliefs and one's sensory and other experiences, as well as comprehensive coherence between first-order experiences, beliefs, and other mental states, on one side, and on the other beliefs *about* first-order states.

We may well ask about certain aspects of broad coherence—e.g., the experience/belief transitions as well as the enumerative and abductive inferences involved—why these should be viewed as adding to the subject's intellectual merit. "Because they are truth-conducive," or at least in good measure for that reason, we are told, "because they increase the likelihood that the subject will have true beliefs and avoid false ones." But that is obviously false of victims in skeptical scenarios, who nevertheless are internally coherent, and even epistemically justified.

Although that seems undeniable, we can perhaps understand it comfortably if we distinguish two sorts of epistemic justification: (a) S is "same-world justified" in believing P in world W iff S believes P in W in virtue of a faculty that *in W* is truth-conducive; and (b) S is "actual-world justified" in believing P in world W iff S believes P in W in virtue of a faculty that *in our actual world* is truth-conducive.

Such relativizing and contextualizing is familiar enough in ordinary thought and speech. Here it enables us to combine the following theses: (a) our broad coherence is necessary for the kind of reflective knowledge traditionally desired; and (b) such broadly coherent knowledge is desirable because in our actual world it helps us approach the truth and avoid error. This is not to deny that there is a kind of "animal knowledge" that owes little to such broad coherence. It is rather only to affirm that beyond "animal knowledge" there is a better knowledge. This reflective knowledge does require a good measure of broad coherence, including one's ability to place one's first-level knowledge in epistemic perspective. But why aspire to any such thing? What is so desirable, epistemically, about broad coherence? We shall return to this in Chapter 10. Let me just note here the benefits of broad coherence through the integrated understanding that it can help us to attain, and for which it is requisite. But broad coherence is also desirable in part because it is truth-conducive (at least conditionally so, in the way of good deduction), *even if in a demon world broad coherence fails this test, and is not truth-conducive*. Even so, *we* can still regard broad coherence as intellectually valuable and admirable so long as we do not regard *our* world as such a world.

We are now, it seems to me, in just the position of arch-internalist Descartes.[13] Descartes considers reasons to doubt, not only one's faculties of perception, memory, and

---

[13] Recall the passage cited earlier: "The fact that an atheist can be 'clearly aware that the three angles of a triangle are equal to two right angles' is something I do not dispute. But I maintain that this awareness of his [*cognitionem*] is not true knowledge [*scientia*], since no act of awareness that can be rendered doubtful seems fit to be called knowledge [*scientia*]. Now since we are supposing that this individual is an atheist, he cannot be certain that he is not being deceived on matters which seem to him to be very evident (as I fully explained). And although this doubt may not occur to him, it can still crop up if someone else raises the point or if he looks into the matter himself. So he will never be free of this doubt until he acknowledges that God exists." This passage is from the Second Set of Replies as it appears in *The Philosophical Writings of Descartes*, ed. J. Cottingham, R. Stoothoff, and D. Murdoch, vol. II, p. 101. However, I must add that where this translation says that an atheist can be "clearly aware," Descartes' Latin is *clare cognoscere*.

introspection, but even one's faculty of intuitive reason, by which one might know that $3 + 2 = 5$, that if one thinks one exists, and the like. And he defends against such doubts by coherence-inducing theological reasoning that yields an epistemic perspective on himself and his world, in terms of which he can feel confident about the reliability of his faculties, *including* the very faculties employed in arriving, via *a priori* theological reasoning, at that perspective on himself and his world, the perspective that enables him to see his world as epistemically propitious.[14]

In *structure* virtue perspectivism is thus Cartesian, though in content it is not. Radical rationalism admits only (rational) intuition and deduction (along with memory) as its faculties of choice (or anyhow of top choice) and wishes to validate all certainty in terms of these faculties. Thus the Cartesian grand project. While broadening our focus beyond certainty to knowledge more broadly, virtue perspectivism admits also perception and introspection, along with intuition and deduction, as well as inductive and abductive reasoning. Gladly using all such faculties, through testimony it accepts also the aid of one's epistemic community. Fortunately, the overview thus attained inspires confidence in the means used.

Rejected as viciously circular by Descartes's critics, and by many today, our procedure does present a troubling aspect of circularity. However, a closer look may show this to be only an illusion.[15]

---

[14] Although unremarked by Descartes, the role of dreams in his perception skepticism is analogous to a role assignable to paradoxes and aporias in a parallel skepticism vis-à-vis rational intuition.

[15] See Chapter 8, above, drawn from "Philosophical Skepticism and Epistemic Circularity," *Proceedings of the Aristotelian Society Supplementary Volume* (1994); and

VI. Epistemic Circularity: What's the Problem?

"I am a thinking being," says Descartes, adding: "Here at last is something I really know. But what is it about this knowledge that makes it knowledge? As far as I can see, it is knowledge because it is a clear and distinct intuition. But it would not be real knowledge unless such intuition were reliable. So I can already lay it down as a general rule that clear and distinct intuition *is* reliable."

"Here is a hand," says G. E. Moore, adding: "Here is something I really know. But what gives me this knowledge? As far as I can see, it is knowledge in virtue of being a deliverance of perceptual experience. But it would not be knowledge if I were dreaming. So I can already conclude that I am *not* dreaming."

Descartes goes on to buttress the reliability of his rational intuition by developing a theology through vigorous use of that very rational intuition. And Moore can similarly appeal to what he knows about his reliable senses on the basis largely of those very senses.

But isn't any such reasoning circular? Yes, circular it does seem to be, "epistemically circular," let us say. But is it *viciously* circular? Skeptics through the ages *have* so attacked it. Sextus Empiricus already uses the tropes of Agrippa in order to develop the so-called *diallelus*, or "problem of the criterion." And many have followed his lead in a long tradition. Today skepticism cum relativism has spread beyond

compare Barry Stroud's response, "Scepticism, 'Externalism', and the Goal of Epistemology," ibid.

epistemology and ethics, beyond philosophy, and even beyond the academy, and its champions often wield circularity as a weapon. But, again: Is such circularity vicious? To say that it is vicious, in the present context, is to say that it is somehow bad, intellectually bad, that it puts us in a situation that is somehow intellectually unsatisfactory. When we ask how the circularity is vicious, therefore, what we want to know is just how it puts us in an unsatisfactory state: when we reason in the way alleged to be viciously circular, wherein lies the defect in our reasoning or in the resulting state?

Largely through the use of rational intuition, Descartes supports the view that rational intuition is reliable and that through its exercise he knows that he thinks and exists.

Largely through the use of perception, Moore could support the view that perception is reliable, that he is *not* misled by a dream, and that through the exercise of perception he knows of the hand before him.

If a crystal ball claims itself to be reliable, then, largely through the crystal ball, a crystal-ball gazer could support the view that such gazing is reliable, that it is rarely misleading, and that through the crystal ball he can foretell the future.

Epistemic circularity is vicious, it might be said, because it would make the gazer as well justified as Descartes or Moore. *Since* there is no way to support adequately the view that intuition is reliable, or that perception is reliable, without employing those very faculties; and *since* the same goes for memory, deduction, abduction, and testimony; *therefore* there is no way to arrive at an acceptable theory of our knowledge and its general sources.

Perhaps that shows only how defective is the attempt to develop such a general theory of one's knowledge and it sources. There *is* an easy way to avoid the intellectual discomfort of having to use a faculty in answering the question whether that faculty is reliable: namely, not to ask the question. Call this the avoidance strategy.

Of course, we will hardly lack company if we avoid philosophy because we find it frustrating. But the avoidance strategy that I wish to consider is not just a rejection of what seems too difficult for one's own intelligence. The implication of the avoidance strategy is not that there is something lacking in one's intelligence but that there is something wrong with the questions avoided.

Much might indeed be wrong with our very general, philosophical questions. Many find them too abstract, too impractical, too useless, and so on. But these are *not* the concerns of *our* avoidance strategist. He is after all a *philosopher*. His concern is not that the questions are just too hard for his intelligence, nor is it their abstractness, impracticality, or uselessness. He would hardly have gone into philosophy with *such* concerns, nor are they his concerns now. Difficulty, abstractness, impracticality, and uselessness are not in his view disqualifying drawbacks.

Why then should one as philosopher avoid questions of epistemology, such as those about the reliability of one's faculties? These questions become pressing with the realization that only if they reliably yield truth can our faculties yield knowledge. This is not just a commitment peculiar to contemporary reliabilism. Indeed, it is found already in Descartes, according to whom intuition (and clear and distinct perception) yields knowledge only if reliable.

Consider a principle of exclusion as follows (where 'excludes' means 'knows not to be the case'):

PE If one is to know that p then one must exclude (rule out) every possibility that one knows to be incompatible with one's knowing that p.[16]

On the basis of PE, we can see that, in order to know that p, one must know that the faculties employed in arriving at one's belief that p are reliable faculties. After all, just consider the possibility that one's operative faculties be unreliable. That is surely a possibility generally known to be incompatible with attaining knowledge through them. Unreliable mechanisms of belief acquisition will not yield knowledge.

If the principle of exclusion is right, therefore, one cannot possibly know that p unless one knows that the faculties involved are reliable. But this is just the sort of knowledge that we seem able to attain only through epistemically circular reasoning.

One might of course question the principle of exclusion.[17] One might hold that in order to know that p one's pertinent faculties need only *be* reliable; one need not *know* them to be reliable. One might for example appeal to a conception of knowledge as mere tracking. One might grant Rorty that causation should not be confused with justification, while joining Nozick in taking tracking as the essence of knowledge, by arguing as follows: "To know *is* just to mirror (or to track) nature. *Justification* is quite another matter. Justification of some sort may well require the principle of

---

[16] Chapter 1 of Stroud's *The Significance of Philosophical Scepticism* is an illuminating discussion of this principle and its importance for understanding philosophical skepticism. In Lecture 6 of *A Virtue Epistemology*, Vol. I of this two-volume work, I suggest how to derive it from other principles with independent plausibility.

[17] For one thing, as it stands it leads, apparently, to a vicious regress. But that is an illusion. After all, what PE requires one to rule out is, *not* every possibility incompatible with one's knowing that p, but rather every possibility *known* to be thus incompatible. Since, for one thing, knowledge requires belief, the regress is hence not infinite, nor does it seem vicious.

exclusion. Thus it may be that in order to be *justified* in believing that p, one must exclude every possibility one knows to be incompatible with one's knowing that p. But *such* justification is *not* required for simple knowledge."

That response seems essentially right. What is more, even Descartes would agree. For Descartes, you will recall, our knowledge that our faculties are reliable, *even* our faculty of reason, depends on our knowledge of God's epistemic good will. Yet Descartes grants explicitly that the atheist mathematician *can* know some mathematics—as we have seen.

The knowledge of an atheist is said to be *cognitio*, however, a second-class accomplishment by comparison with *scientia*. *Scientia*, by contrast, *does* require relevant knowledge of one's reliability. Only thus can one repel doubts about the possible unreliability of one's faculties. Only thus can one exclude a possibility evidently incompatible with one's knowing that p: namely, the possibility that only unreliable faculties yield one's belief.

By analogy we can more generally distinguish *animal* knowledge, which requires only that one track nature, on one hand, and on the other *reflective* knowledge, which requires also awareness of *how* one knows, in a way that precludes the unreliability of one's faculties. Unlike Descartes' *cognitio* and *scientia*, our more general animal and reflective knowledge do not require *infallible* reliability, but only a high level of reliability.[18]

The avoidance strategy now has not only the cost of suppressing philosophical curiosity about knowledge. We can

---

[18] This distinction figures in my *Knowledge in Perspective* (Cambridge: Cambridge University Press, 1991); see, e.g., pp. 240 and 282.

now see how it *also* precludes first-level *reflective* knowledge, and of course *scientia*. Given these costs, what again counts in favor of avoidance? So far we have been told that we must avoid epistemic circularity because it entails arriving at a generally positive view of one's faculties only by use of those very faculties. But why should that be frustrating when it is the inevitable consequence of its generality. So far the answer is only that the superstitious crystal-gazer could reason analogously and with equal justification in defense of his own perspective. How damaging is this?

Suppose we grant the gazer epistemic justification and internal coherence equal to our own. Still, internal coherence is clearly insufficient. Isn't that obvious in view of paranoia, hypochondria, and similar psychoses? Logical brilliance permits logical coherence but does not even ensure sanity, much less general epistemic aptitude. There are faculties other than reason whose apt functioning is also crucial to the subject's epistemic welfare.

In light of that result, why not distinguish between the gazers and the perceivers in that, although both *reason* properly and attain thereby coherence and justification, only the perceivers are more fully epistemically competent and attain knowledge?

On this view, the crystal-gazers differ from the perceivers in that gazing is not reliable while perceiving is. So the theory of knowledge of the perceivers is right, that of the gazers wrong. Moreover, the perceivers *can* know their theory to be right when they know it in large part through perception, since their theory *is* right and perception *can* thus serve as a source of knowledge. The gazers are by hypothesis in a very different position. Gazing, being *un*reliable, cannot serve as a source of knowledge. So the perceivers have a good source or basis for their knowledge, but the gazers, lacking any such source or basis, lack knowledge.

Still one might insist that the perceivers should not be so smug. They should still feel acute discomfort and intellectual frustration. This I find a very widely shared view, in epistemology and, *mutatis mutandis*, far beyond. We have seen, for example, how, according to Barry Stroud, the perceivers can at best reach a position where they can affirm the conditional proposition that *if* their perception is reliable, *then* they know.[19] And he has more recently reemphasized what is essentially the same thesis as follows:

. . . Sosa's "externalist" could say at most: "If the theory I hold is true, I do know or have good reason to believe that I know or have good reason to believe it, and I do understand how I know the things I do." I think . . . we can see a way in which the satisfaction the theorist seeks in understanding his knowledge still eludes him. Given that all of his knowledge of the world is in question, he will still find himself able to say only "I might understand my knowledge, I might not. Whether I do or not all depends on how things in fact are in the world I think I've got knowledge of".[20]

However, it is not easy to understand this position. If our perceivers believe (a) that their perception, *if* reliable, yields them knowledge, and (b) that their perception *is* reliable, then why are they restricted to affirming only the conditional, *a*, and not its antecedent, *b*? Why must they *wonder whether* they understand their relevant knowledge? Indeed, to the extent that they are really convinced of *both a and b*, it would

[19] See "Understanding Human Knowledge in General," in M. Clay and K. Lehrer (eds.), *Knowledge and Scepticism* (Boulder: Westview, 1989), p. 47.
[20] B. Stroud, "Scepticism, 'Externalism', and the Goal of Epistemology," op. cit., pp. 303–4.

seem that, far from being logically constrained *to* wondering whether they know, they are, on the contrary, logically constrained *from* so wondering. After all, first, if you are really *certain* that p, then you cannot well consider whether you know it without thinking that you do. Moreover, second, isn't it incoherent to be convinced that p *and yet* wonder whether p?

In sum, I see no sufficient reason to settle *either* for irresoluble frustration *or* for the avoidance strategy. The main argument we have seen for that depends on the claim that if we allow the circular defense offered for externalist epistemology, then the gazers turn out no less epistemically justified than the perceivers. In a sense that is true: but then in a sense they *are* equally internally justified, equally coherent. Nevertheless, they are *not* equally adroit or apt in all epistemically relevant respects. Perception is of course reliable while gazing is not. Therefore, the perceivers are right and competent both in their particular perceptual beliefs, at least generally, *and* in their theory of knowledge—for it all rests in large measure on their reliable perception. By contrast, the gazers are wrong (maladroit and inapt) both in their particular gaze-derived beliefs and in *their* theory of knowledge—for it all rests on their *un*reliable gazing. Moreover, I see no reason why the perceivers must be restricted to affirming only the conditional that *if* perception is reliable then they know. I see no reason why they cannot also affirm the antecedent, why they cannot believe, both rationally and aptly, that perception *is* reliable and does enable them to know.

VII. Circles Beyond Belief

Why require the appeal to comprehensive enough coherence for justification, an appeal that I have attributed to Descartes, as part of what justifies his recourse to theology in accounting for true knowledge (*scientia*)? Why not say that what justifies is that one's beliefs be caused by the gods? And if the question arises, why not add that *this* belief itself is justified because it is itself caused by the gods? We *could* of course proceed in this simplified way without worrying about coherence or about the source of these beliefs beyond attributing them to divine agency. But that is not the way we are built, most of us: we just do not acquire such beliefs the way we do acquire beliefs willy-nilly when we open our eyes in good light. But what if we *were* built that way? Would we then be justified in having such beliefs, and in explaining our justification for having them, by their origin in divine agency? Would we then be justified to the degree and in the way in which Descartes is justified or in the way in which our imagined Moore would be justified through his appeal to a more ordinary reliabilism than that of Descartes? Internally regarded, the structure of beliefs would share prominent features in all three cases. Of course, from our Moorean, commonsense position we can object both to Cartesianism and to the invocation of the gods. These views are internally coherent, but we might still reject them as wrong. And we might be able to explain what is wrong with them, from our point of view, especially if our point of view rules out their leading ideas. But they can, for their part, return the favor. Besides, we can anyhow imagine someone brilliant but insane, who weaves a system of immense interlocking complexity, but one wholly detached from reality as we know it commonsensically. Such a madman could object to our commonsense beliefs in a way that would seem relevantly analogous to the way in which we would object to his mad beliefs.

What all of that shows, it seems to me, is nothing more than that knowledge does not live by coherence and truth alone. Knowledge requires truth and coherence, true enough, but it often requires more: e.g., that one be adequately related, causally or counterfactually, to the objects of one's knowledge, which is not necessarily ensured by the mere truth-cum-coherence of one's beliefs, no matter how comprehensive the coherence. Madmen can be richly, brilliantly coherent; not just imaginary madmen, but real ones, some of them locked up in asylums. Knowledge requires not only internal justification or coherence or rationality, but also external warrant or aptness. We must be *both* in good internal order *and* in appropriate relation to the external world.

VIII. The Sosa/Stroud Dialectic: A Further Twist[21]

Stroud doubts that we can attain a philosophically satisfying account of our knowledge of the external world if we think that our knowledge is based on but goes beyond what lies open to our direct awareness. If we view our perceptual knowledge as does the indirect realist, then we are hard put to see how we could gain any such philosophically satisfying understanding. This is brought home if we compare our situation with that of a crystal ball gazer who thinks that what he can see in the ball enables him to tell about matters beyond. Such beliefs could be reliably acquired if their subject matter were suitably related to what can be seen in the ball. Similarly, on the indirect realist picture we can know about

---

[21] A more recent installment in this debate is Stroud's contribution to John Greco (ed.), *Ernest Sosa and His Critics* (Oxford: Blackwell, 2004); what follows presents Stroud's further critique along with my reply.

external reality if the experiential basis for such beliefs is suitably related to their subject matter. In each case, *if* there is a suitable relation between our basis and what we believe on that basis, then our beliefs repose truth-reliably on that basis. But if we do not know that there is such a relation between our basis and what we believe on that basis, then we attain no philosophically satisfying understanding of how we know on that basis.

It is hard to disagree with that analysis. If our acceptance of an account of a certain subject matter is to give us real understanding of that subject matter, then it must at a minimum be true, but more than that it must be something we know to be true. Mere beliefs about how people know what they do will not constitute understanding, will not give "a satisfactory explanation of human perceptual knowledge." Moreover,

. . . even knowing that people know things in that way would not be enough, if knowing is simply a matter of fulfilling the conditions Sosa's theory says are sufficient for knowledge. All the theorist can appeal to in accounting for his own knowledge as more than confident belief are the perceptual experiences he knows he has had, the beliefs he holds, which he believes to be the result of those experiences, and the theory of knowledge that he also believes. That theory says that *if* one further condition holds, then he does know what he thinks he knows. And he believes that that further condition holds. But still he remains in no better position for understanding himself as knowing what he thinks he knows than someone who reflects on his knowledge with equal confidence and in an equally satisfactory way and yet knows nothing at all.

Or so we are told; and here we have reached the distinctive core of Stroud's particular form of skeptical doubt. About his distinctive view, we must ask: Why might it be that even our knowledge that people know things in a certain way would still not yield philosophically satisfying understanding of how they know? Why is it that the theory we know to be true as to how it is that they know still fails to give us any such understanding?

The question is whether holding such a theory leaves anyone in a position to gain a satisfactory understanding of knowledge of the world, even if he fulfills the conditions Sosa's theory says are sufficient for knowledge. Could someone in such a position come to recognize himself as knowing, and not merely confidently believing, perhaps even truly, that sense perception is a way of getting knowledge of the world and crystal ball gazing is not?

I think that, on the understanding of perception that appears to be involved in Sosa's question . . ., the answer is "No". On that view, what we are aware of in perception is restricted to features of our perceptual experiences. The external facts we know as a result of those experiences are nothing we ever perceive to be so. What we get in sense perception therefore bears the same relation to the world we think we know by that means as what is seen in crystal ball gazing bears to the world the gazers think it gives them knowledge of.

We do believe that our perceptual experiences are reliably connected with what we think we know on their basis.

But anyone who thinks that all it takes to have satisfactory understanding of perceptual knowledge is to conclude by *modus ponens* that we know by perception that there are external things would have to concede that the crystal ball gazers have a satisfactory understanding of crystal ball gazing knowledge. They could draw the corresponding conclusion equally confidently from what they believe about themselves.

Remarkably, this is said to be so despite the fact that, while the contents of our experiences *are* reliably connected with the beliefs that they yield, the contents of the crystal balls have *no* reliable connection with the truth of their deliverances. Thus ". . . there are no reliable connections between what people see in crystal balls and what goes on in the world beyond them. If the gazers could raise their eyes from their crystal balls and see what is so in the world around them, they could see that too." So, while we can know our perceptual beliefs to be reliably formed, the gazers cannot know their gaze-derived beliefs to be thus reliable, and cannot know that they know things about the world around them by basing them on any such reliable basis.

Stroud's reasoning now is hard to follow. He had explicitly granted, at least for the sake of argument, my externalist account of knowledge. So his doubts do not target that account. He is willing to assume that perceptual knowledge is a matter of perceptual beliefs prompted truth-reliably by perceptual experiences. How then can he coherently suppose that if we conclude by *modus ponens* that we know about the world around us through perception, given that our perceptual faculties are reliable, then we are in the predicament he alleges? He alleges that we then ". . . would have to concede that the crystal ball gazers have a satisfactory understanding of crystal ball gazing knowledge. They could draw the corresponding conclusion equally confidently from what they believe about themselves." But this is refuted by a crucial difference that Stroud and I both recognize: namely, that we know our perceptual faculties to be reliable whereas the gazers believe but do not know their gazing to be reliable. So, how can we be in an equally good epistemic position to understand how we know, if we *do* know but they *do not* know about the reliability of the faculties involved?

Stroud in any case rejects my appeal to a reliable sensory basis for understanding how our perceptual beliefs can constitute knowledge, and indeed traces to that particular feature of my account its failure as a philosophically satisfying account of our perceptual knowledge. His preferred account would explain rather that we can often enough just directly see *that we can see* some external fact to be so, and that we can in this way know how we know about the world around us. Circularity is here no threat, since circularity occurs in reasoning, and here there is no reasoning, but only plain seeing.

I find three problems with this interesting approach. Let us grant, first, that some perceptual knowledge is direct in not depending on other perceptual knowledge or distinguishable perceptual experience. Even so, our knowledge that someone else knows something perceptually does not seem plausibly a case in point. Second, even if *sometimes* we know how others know the world around them because we perceive, for some external fact, *that they perceive it* (that they perceive that external fact), perception is not the only source of our knowledge of the external world. Unaided perception is, on the contrary, a very limited source of such knowledge, if we consider the vast bulk of our stored knowledge, and the dependence of this knowledge on the likes of inference, memory, and testimony. So it remains to be seen how we can know about our general possession of such knowledge, including our nonperceptual knowledge. We would hardly be able to perceive directly that we enjoy much of our mnemonic or inferential or testimonial knowledge.

That gives rise to a third problem for Stroud, whose reasoning culminates as follows.

The conclusion I would draw from all this is that in order to achieve a satisfactory understanding of our knowledge of the world we must set aside or overcome the idea that the deliverances of perception even at its best are limited to the character of one's perceptual experiences alone. . . . Perceptual knowledge of external things is seen [in externalist accounts like Sosa's] as a combination of some prior knowledge which is not knowledge of external things plus something else. That is what I think leaves us in the plight I have described.

The further problem for Stroud concerns the vast bulk of our knowledge that, while based on perceptual knowledge concurrent or past, is not itself perceptual knowledge. A lot of our knowledge *is* after all in some way a "combination" of some prior knowledge plus something else. Moreover, the supporting facts now or earlier perceived to be so and the knowledge supported at one or another remove by our perception of those facts, are not generally connected in ways that we can see or otherwise perceive. If we recall the main objection brought by Stroud against externalist reliabilism concerning perception, his own view seems now ironically subject to that same objection. For the vast bulk of our knowledge of the external world presumably goes beyond the perceptual knowledge on which at some depth it is based, and yet we cannot just perceive that the content of that knowledge is related appropriately to the perceptual knowledge that forms its basis. It remains to be seen how, despite that fact, we do know all those things about the world around us that we know non-perceptually, and how we can know in a philosophically satisfying way that we do have any such knowledge.[22]

Can we do so while avoiding vicious circularity, and, if so, how so? We turn next to these questions.

---

[22] For perception-transcendent, reason-dependent knowledge, then, we would seem to face three choices. Either we deny that there is any, or we affirm that there is some but deny that we can ever attain any philosophically satisfying understanding of it; otherwise, we must after all face the issue of vicious circularity.

Chapter 10

Easy Knowledge and the Criterion*

Consider the following proposition:[1]

KR A potential knowledge source K can yield knowledge for S, only if S knows that K is reliable.

If we *affirm* KR, we face the problem of vicious circularity. How can we attain the required knowledge that our epistemic sources are reliable? Must we not *have* that knowledge *already* before the sources can deliver it to us? How can we know perception to be reliable, for example, without basing our belief on our empirical knowledge derived ultimately from perception? And the same goes for memory and other sources.

If we *deny* KR, that apparently enables us to bootstrap our way from the deliverances of a source on some occasion (or upon a series of them) to conclusions about the safety of its operation on that occasion (or about its general reliability). But this is clearly unacceptable.

The problem thus sketched, we begin with a closer look at the content of KR.

* The contents of this chapter derive from work long in (slow) progress, presented most recently at an Arché conference and a Wisconsin workshop, at both of which I benefited from helpful discussion.

[1] This is the key proposition in Stewart Cohen's statement of the problem, in "Basic Knowledge and the Problem of Easy Knowledge," *Philosophy and Phenomenological Research* 65, 2 (2002): 309–29.

I. On Sources

One might object to KR by pointing out how difficult it is to specify the sources of some most clearly known propositions: the proposition that one exists, for example, or that either something exists or not. As things stand, a defender of KR can respond that indeed it *is* difficult to specify such sources, since there are none. This is in fact rather plausible if we think of an epistemic source for a belief Bp as a basis for that belief, something that the belief is based on, some reason for which the believer believes as he does. Perhaps some beliefs have no such basis, and need none. Indeed, the beliefs just highlighted are plausible examples. However, if even these beliefs turn out to have a rational basis, they will then after all have a source, the source constituted by the basis. Accordingly, if most of our knowledge is constituted by beliefs that require supporting reasons in order to be properly held, that suffices to make KR interesting. For it now specifies a necessary condition for the bulk of our knowledge: that is, for all such knowledge that requires reasons (operative either at the given time when the knowledge is present, or at some earlier time in its aetiology).

The notion of a source of knowledge might still be deemed problematic, nevertheless, so as to weaken any principle that makes use of it, such as KR. But the notion is not so unclear as to render the principle unacceptable or uninteresting. Again, one could understand what it is to be a "source" of a belief as just to be a "basis" for that belief, something that the belief is based on. Even evidentialists who focus on propositional justification make use of this notion. They do so, for example, in explaining their concept of a "well-founded" belief as one

held "on the basis of" some body of evidence. This is said
to be not only evidence one "has" but also evidence one
"uses" in holding the attitude. KR can even be rephrased
so as to use the notion of a "basis" rather than that of a
"source," with the dialectic then proceeding more or less as
before.[2]

A specific belief B might be formed in a *token* rational way
W, where W is of a causally relevant type W′, such that when
any belief B of that representational *sort* is formed in that same
type of causal way W′ (where the same intrinsic or relational

---

[2] If the relevant sort of basis here is a *rational* basis, one that constitutes or has
as content a *reason* for which one believes as one does, how might such a basis
function as a source? Well, "basis" and "source" are metaphors, explicable in
terms of dependence or causation or explanation, so that the rational basis of a
belief would be a reason for which the belief is held, a reason that *motivates* that
belief (or helps to do so, either now or earlier in its aetiology). But what more
specifically might be involved in the *reliability* of such a rational basis or motive
for belief?

It is clearly epistemic reliability that is at issue, and here we focus on truth-
reliability. So, the "reliability" of our epistemic sources, as now understood, is
the reliability of a rational basis in getting us to the truth. All right, but what,
more specifically, is involved in this? Well, if the basis R is a psychological state
of the believer's, then presumably it motivates the further psychological state, the
belief B, in virtue of some of its specific features. These will be features causally
relevant to the believer's hosting that particular token belief at that time, with its
specific representational content.

Still, what might it mean to say that the source, the rational basis, is truth-
reliable, if the source is a token psychological state that helps cause the belief
token B? That the source is thus truth-reliable would presumably mean that the
belief B, with its particular representational content, is (sufficiently) likely to be
true given that it is thus causally based. This all concerns a particular pair of
token states, however, one of them a belief with a certain content, a belief likely
to be true given that it is caused by the other token state (itself a belief or an
experience), in virtue of certain features of the latter. How do we get from all
this to a more general "source," something that might be assessed for reliability?
Pretty clearly we would need the belief to have a *sort* of representational content,
and we would need the rational basis R to have causally relevant features, such
that when a belief with *such* representational content is rationally motivated by a
basis, in virtue of *such* features of that basis, the belief tends to be true (provided
the basis is true or veridical).

features of that way of forming beliefs are causally operative), then B tends to be true. Here W is the token source or rational basis or rational way of forming or sustaining belief B, whereas W′ is the general type under which that token relevantly falls. Suppose W contains the entire rational basis bearing motivationally on B, all the specific reasons that bear on the subject's rational motivation for holding that belief B. In that case, if B is to amount to knowledge, then the relevant source type W′ corresponding to that token source must be truth-reliable: i.e., beliefs rationally formed (reason-based) in that type of way must tend to be true.[3]

There is however an alternative to thinking of sources as necessarily involving rational bases.[4] We could instead retreat to a more general conception of an epistemic competence. Some competences operate on rational inputs and deliver

---

[3] To specify what makes a source type "relevant" would be to solve a sort of generality problem. Here I will not offer a solution; I'll suggest only an indication of what seems required: Suppose S takes himself to see something red and triangular, where S's reason for holding that token belief is that it looks to him as if he sees something red and triangular (while nothing in his background beliefs or present experience suggests that the situation is "fishy"). Here a relevant source type might be as follows: (a) its looking to S as if he sees something F and G, for basic perceptible characteristics F and G (where nothing in S's background beliefs or experiences suggests that his situation is relevantly "fishy"), provided (b) in general if something were to look thus to S (etc.) that would motivate S to believe that he sees something F and G. The factors concerning S's mental state that help constitute the source type are those that would motivate S to hold a belief with the relevant sort of content (the sort that abstracts from such particulars as the indexically or demonstratively picked out time of that particular belief (token). The epistemological issues to be confronted here require no prior solution to relevant generality problems, and it would be distracting to tarry over such problems. In brief, we can think of the relevant sources as rational bases, whether token or type. Accordingly, KR can be understood as follows: S's belief that p can constitute knowledge, when that belief is fully based on a complete token motivating rationale R, only if S knows the relevant rationale type R′ (of which R is a token) to be reliable.

[4] The terminology of 'basing' and its cognates in this paper will be short for 'rational basing' or 'basing on reasons that motivate what is thus based'.

outputs on that basis. These are reliable dispositions to believe correctly based on the rational inputs (and conditionally on their truth). We might allow, however, that some beliefs can be epistemically justified without being based on reasons. Not every belief lacking a rational basis will be epistemically justified, surely, so we must then distinguish those that are *properly* formed even with no basis, such as perhaps the simplest beliefs of logic or arithmetic, from possible superstitious beliefs deprived of a rational basis *without* being properly formed and sustained. The competently held intuitive beliefs of logic or arithmetic, can then be distinguished, among others, from the equally baseless beliefs that are nothing better than ill-formed superstition.[5]

If we interpret KR in this alternative way, then the sources whose reliability is at issue in KR would be such competences of the believer's, some of them rational competences to base beliefs properly on adroit weighing of the reasons pro or con, whereas other sources would involve no such basing, but would still involve either belief-forming or belief-sustaining competences, though ones sensitive to the sheer contents believed, without reliance on ulterior reasons.[6]

---

[5] Here it is left open that some or all such beliefs be innate, implausible though that seems for most or even all of them. Whether innate or not, something seats the abilities humans have to hold such beliefs, distinguishing them from lower animals or, for that matter, rocks. Moreover, humans can acquire superstitious beliefs through malign social pressure rather than through reasons. Such superstitious beliefs, unlike those of, say, arithmetic, where social pressure may also be operative, are *not* formed through socially-cum-individually-seated *competence*.

[6] It might be thought that so-called baseless rational beliefs must after all be based at least on understanding of the propositions believed. True, but that is a universal necessary condition for the formation of a belief: one must always understand the proposition believed. It is not, however, just the understanding of a proposition that gives a proper basis for believing it. Otherwise, it would be also a basis for believing its negation, which must be equally well understood.

Although that is a more general conception of sources, in what follows we focus initially on *rational* sources, where the competence exercised is that of forming and holding beliefs based on reasons motivating them *at that very moment*. This may assuage concerns about our access to the sources of our beliefs.[7]

What suffices is rather the being understood (shared by a proposition and its negation pretty much equally) *along with the specific content of that very proposition.* It is hard to go beyond this to some *general* feature, however, which, when combined with the being understood, will properly yield acceptance. Simplicity cannot plausibly be such a feature, for example, since, again, a proposition will never be that much simpler than its negation. (And besides it is often the more complicated negation that is intuitively justified.) Nevertheless, something distinguishes the simple truths of arithmetic, for example, making them suitable objects of immediate acceptance upon understanding, and giving them their attraction to normal human minds universally (upon understanding). Whatever it is, whether innate or socially instilled, the outcome is uniform and general enough to suggest some sort of disposition at work (whether wholly individually seated, or partially socially seated). Given how epistemically benign it is, finally, this disposition seems not inappropriately considered a "competence."

[7] When your belief is based on reasons, is motivated by them, you tend to have access to the fact that those are your reasons, even if the access is not universal or automatic, and may even be fraught in certain cases. Thus, in certain cases you might lack knowledge, or at least knowledge of an important, reflective, sort, precisely because you lack such access. Other sorts of epistemic sources might be defined. For example, we might allow sources of normative status. On this conception an epistemic source—and indeed a sort of "source" of knowledge—would be whatever property of a belief might constitute the base on which its relevant normative property (e.g., that of being epistemically justified) might supervene. But here we will work for now with the conception of sources as rational bases. Thus, in one sense (the one to be used here for now) the "source" of one's knowledge would be the rational basis of the constitutive belief, whereas in another sense the epistemic "source" of one's knowledge would be the source of the epistemic justification of the constitutive belief, and this would be the belief's *having* the rational basis that *is* in the earlier sense its source (and thereby a source of the knowledge, when the belief does amount to knowledge). In his paper "Externalism, Skepticism, and the Problem of Easy Knowledge" (*The Philosophical Review* 114 (2005): 33–61), José Zalabardo discusses a problem of easy knowledge that is related to ours, and to Cohen's, but is different in two respects: first, it focuses on warrant where ours focuses on knowledge; second, the warrant it focuses on is propositional rather than doxastic; at least, it is a

The concerns are fueled anew, however, by the following fact: that the vast bulk of our present beliefs are not ones we hold for sufficient reasons *motivationally operative at this very moment when they are held* (mostly in storage). What is more, the vast bulk of these beliefs are ones whose rational aetiology is now beyond our ability to recall. So, for this vast bulk, it is hard to see how we could presently know their sources to be reliable, since we now lack access to what those sources *are*.[8]

However that may turn out, it will not solve the problem of easy knowledge, since the problem takes the form of a dilemma, *each* horn of which has been argued to be problematic. If we say that in many cases we know while blind to how reliable our sources may be, we still have the following problematic implication: namely, that we need only find out what those sources are in order to *learn* that they are reliable, either by being safe in that specific instance where the given belief is held, or by being generally reliable, when we bootstrap to this conclusion.

In any case, let us focus here more specifically on the cases wherein our belief has a rational source motivationally operative at the time when the belief is held. Even restricting the quantificational scope of KR to such beliefs, we have prima facie a problem of easy knowledge as sketched at the outset. Let us take up this restricted problem.

warrant that a proposition can have for a subject regardless of whether the subject then believes the proposition, or has any propositional attitude to it. It is different from our problem here in both respects, and different from Cohen's problem in at least the first respect. These differences are important enough to make the two (or possibly three) problems substantially different problems.

[8] This is not to say that you must always know the source of a belief in order to know that the source of that belief, whatever it may be, must be reliable. Compare here Moore's reasoning against the skeptic. Nevertheless, there is special reason for concern that in too many cases we may be unable to know our source to be reliable, if in all such cases we cannot even know what our source *is*.

So, here's the plan. Let's focus on reason-based competences or faculties,[9] which form or sustain a belief based on reasons motivationally operative at the time when the belief is held. Let's not try to decide which sources specifically operate thus, while allowing that at least our perceptual faculties tend to operate that way. Special sub-issues of the problem of easy knowledge arise for these faculties or sources, sub-issues worth discussing on their own. So that is what I propose we do. More general issues may arise for our competences generally, whether reason-based or not. But let us shelve any such issues for now, returning to them eventually.[10]

II. What Must We Presuppose in Properly Trusting a Source? What Epistemic Status is Required in Such a Presupposition?

Here again is the key principle:

KR A potential knowledge source K can yield knowledge for S, only if S knows that K is reliable.

The denial of this principle is said to allow for "basic" knowledge, knowledge delivered by a source that the subject does not know to be reliable, which creates a problem as follows:

The problem . . . arises from denying the KR principle whether the theory that denies it is evidentialist or non-evidentialist. If you allow for basic knowledge, there is nothing to stop us from acquiring, by trivial inferences, all sorts of knowledge about how we are

---

[9] Faculties seem highly generic competences: thus compare the epistemic competences of a bird watcher with the faculty of perception.

[10] This chapter will focus first on reason-based competences, only later to take up competences generally, whether reason-based or not.

not deceived or misled by our belief sources.[11] But intuitively this knowledge seems available only if we have prior knowledge about the world—knowledge not required by the views in question.[12]

Here's how this works in a particular case. If a wall looks red, based on which you know it to be red, you are then able to deduce that it is *not* white with misleading lights shining on it. *If* your knowledge that the wall is red is basic knowledge, accordingly, delivered just by your taking how it looks at face value, *then* you seem enabled to deduce that the wall is not white but illuminated with misleading lights, *and* to discover thereby this previously unknown fact. Why does this seem so clearly unacceptable?

Of course, even if KR is false it may still be that in order for you to know that the wall is red it is not enough to base your belief that it is red simply on its looking red. Perhaps your belief must be based on that visual appearance *along with a presupposition that your situation is relevantly unproblematic.* Moreover, one cannot simply install that presupposition at will, *arbitrarily*, and expect thereby to acquire epistemically justified beliefs. One's presuppositions must have appropriate epistemic status; they must themselves be epistemically "justified." Suppose, indeed, that in order to *know* that the wall is red based on taking its look at face value, you must presuppose your situation to be relevantly unproblematic. In that case, you must then *appropriately* (*epistemically* appropriately, perhaps *knowledgeably*) presuppose that it is thus *un*problematic. And this implies that you cannot then *posteriorly acquire* this

---

[11] Is this knowledge of the reliability of our faculties? Not in any modal sense. It is only knowledge that in this particular instance one is not deceived.

[12] Cohen, "Basic Knowledge and the Problem of Easy Knowledge", 315–16. Cf.: "The problem is that once we allow for basic knowledge, we can acquire reliability knowledge very easily—in fact, all too easily, from an intuitive perspective" (p. 311).

appropriateness (amounting perhaps to knowledge), based on the knowledge that presupposes it, namely the knowledge that the wall is then red. This would explain why it seems so clearly wrong to suppose that we could *discover* in the way suggested that the wall is not white but illuminated with misleading lights. For, if in knowing the wall to be red you must knowledgeably presuppose that the lights are not misleading, then you must already virtually know that the wall is not white under misleading light. After all, this is a bit of knowledge already implicitly contained in your know-ledgeable presupposition that the light is not misleading. So it could not possibly come as a complete discovery drawn as a conclusion from your knowledge that the wall was red. This helps explain why it seems so implausible that we could properly make any such epistemically productive inference. But let us have a closer look.

Suppose that, in order to know the wall to be red in the first place, by taking its looking red at face value, one must justifiedly *presuppose* P, that one's situation "permits" taking such an appearance at face value—i.e., that it is not a situation where such an appearance might too easily be misleading. This presupposition, P, entails that the wall is not illuminated by misleading light. Can one on this basis therefore *deny* that the wall is both white and illuminated by misleading light? Surely one cannot *knowledgeably* issue this denial *based simply on such knowledge that the wall is red*. If knowing that the wall is red requires one to presuppose one's situation not to be mis-leading, it requires one to presuppose this not just arbitrarily but with appropriate epistemic standing. Accordingly, even *if* presupposition P need not be installed *with priority*, still at a minimum it cannot possibly derive its standing *posteriorly* to the knowledge that requires it as a presupposition.

Do we now have a solution to the problem of easy knowledge? Does our reasoning provide a way to deny KR while denying also that one can come to know *that the wall is not white under misleading light* through a trivial inference from one's knowledge that the wall is red?

Well, might the following two things be true conjointly?

(a) KR is false: in particular, a potential knowledge source K *can* give one knowledge that the wall one sees is red, despite one's *not* then knowing that K is truth-reliable.

(b) One cannot know the wall to be red by taking one's visual experience at face value unless (i) in believing the wall to be red one *presupposes correctly and justifiedly that one's situation is trustworthy for judging whether the wall is red through taking the look of things at face value,* and (ii) *in so presupposing one is not doing so arbitrarily, or in some other epistemically defective way.*

The crucial question now concerns the relation between *this* epistemic accomplishment, the one in (b), and knowledge that one's source K is reliable when, on the basis of its look, one believes the wall to be red. Is such "presupposing correctly and justifiedly" a form of *knowing*? If not, how does it differ? Is the "trustworthiness of one's relevant situation for judging whether p" different from the reliability of one's source K for believing that p? If so, just how do they differ? If the presupposing at issue in (b) above must amount to a form of (implicit) knowing, and if "knowing that one's situation is trustworthy for judging whether p" is tantamount to "knowing that one's source for so judging is reliable," then (a) and (b) would seem incompatible.

We wondered whether we had found a way to deny KR and still avoid the outcome that one can come to know *that the wall is not white under misleading light* through a trivial inference from one's knowledge that the wall is red. If (a) and (b) are incompatible, then the answer is in the negative, and we have no solution to the easy knowledge problem after all. *Are* they incompatible? We should pause over this.

Let us first distinguish between conscious, explicit knowledge and implicit knowledge that can be made conscious without leaving the armchair. The presuppositions of interest here are, let us suppose, states of a subject that he can thus bring to consciousness. Must not such presuppositions be true, epistemically well based, and indeed a kind of knowledge (even if implicit)? Consider again the relevant source of one's belief that p. Suppose its relevant trustworthiness to be *epistemic* trustworthiness, a matter of its truth-reliability, so that beliefs *thus* acquired cannot too easily be false. Given these assumptions, the required presupposition plausibly amounts after all to *knowledge* that one's source is reliable. Alternatively, it is something so close to knowledge that the whole dialectic could be recast to similar effect in terms of such *quasi-knowledge*.

What makes it so similar to knowledge? Well, it is after all a kind of propositional attitude, or at least a state that can be described with propositional content, whether one is willing to call it an "attitude" or not.[13] Anyhow, the propositional state that constitutes our "quasi-knowledge" is one that requires its own positive normative standing in order to do its proper epistemic work, a standing subject to the traditional epistemic framework involving: rational basis, Gettierization, truth, defeat, challenge, defense, competence, aptness, etc.

---

[13] Compare the rigid state of an enclosing cage that brings it about that the tiger within is restrained within that space; this is not an attitude of that cage, but it is a state of it that is describable with propositional content, as one that brings it about *that such and such*.

One might well wonder what the crucial difference is, then, that exempts such presuppositions from needing justification of their own, or what might as well be called epistemic justification (or competence, i.e., being an instance of competent presupposing), and from needing even to amount to knowledge, at least animal knowledge, if they are properly to fulfill their epistemic role.[14]

III. Presuppositions Required for Perceptual Knowledge

Can we know the color of a surface simply by taking its appearance at face value? Or do we also need to be positioned

---

[14] Can't we agree that there are dispositions to take visual experience at face value in play when we visually perceive, e.g., that a wall we see is red? Won't there then be a state that is the basis for that disposition, and isn't it plausible to describe the person as being disposed to believe that he sees something red upon having a visual experience as if he does? If so, then won't it be proper to attribute to such a person an implicit "commitment" whose content is something like: "if it looks red, then it is red," an implicit assumption, or presupposition, or mindset, to that effect? This would be analogous to the unspoken and perhaps even unrecognized prejudices of someone who nonetheless makes evident in his conduct that he regards members of a certain target group as inferior.

As I will go on to argue later in the main text, there are competences (dispositions, abilities, intellectual virtues) in play when we acquire and sustain beliefs correctly, and these dispositions require proper epistemic standing if they are to do their proper epistemic justificatory work, and this standing must not all be earned through reasoning based on antecedently justified deliverances of those very faculties. If we can agree on all that, I will argue further that such proper standing can be earned largely through the fact that the dispositions in question are just brutely reliable as part of a normal human's natural endowment, even if that standing can then be boosted through rational means. Thus, it can be boosted through a perspective developed through the deliverances of such animal competences. Once it is thus boosted, it ascends to the level of reflective standing, which means that the belief is now defensible from certain doubts pressed against the alleged competence whence it derives, if any, and against the circumstances of the operation of that competence, and how propitious these are. A belief that is defensible from any such doubts is thereby epistemically superior, and its superiority consists, at least in part, in such defensibility.

to rule out various ways in which such a perceptual claim could be undermined or blocked? Arguably, we might even need evidence for the absence of at least the well-known obstacles or underminers, such as sub-standard capacities and misleading conditions. In any particular case such evidence enables one to infer the veridicality of whatever may be the source of our belief. If our conclusion is neither false nor Gettiered, we thereby attain knowledge. And this knowledge can then form the basis for a further inference that the particular source, however fallible, does not lead us astray in that particular case.[15]

Is that really a way for you to learn that your source does not "fail" you on a particular occasion? What might "failure" amount to here? Correspondingly, what is it for a "source or basis" to be "veridical"?

The sort of implicit knowledge most problematically involved in the problem of easy knowledge takes either of two forms:[16]

---

[15] This is a position defended by Earl Conee, expounded in his paper, "Foundational Epistemology," delivered as a symposium talk for the Pacific APA meetings, 2004, and referenced here by permission.

[16] Suppose we hold a belief Bp that we know to have a source or basis X. What is required for X (or X's deliverance) to be then *veridical*? Is it sufficient that Bp be true, i.e., that $<p>$ be true, i.e., that p? If it *is* enough that $<p>$ be true, then the veridicality of source X (or its deliverance) in yielding belief *Bp is* of course very easy to know, at least once one knows that p. For, one can now reason trivially from

    1. p

and

    2. My belief Bp has source X

to

    3. In yielding my belief Bp, source X is veridical.

Either

it is the knowledge that source X is *generically* reliable with modal force, i.e., *would* lead us aright or would tend to lead us aright with its deliverances;

or else

it is the knowledge that source X is *specifically* reliable with modal force, i.e., *would* lead us aright or would tend to lead us aright in its deliverance in the present instance (not easily would it in that instance lead us astray).

That is to say, at a minimum it must not be the case that source X would now deliver <p> without the slightest sensitivity to whether it is true that p, so that it could *just as easily* have so delivered while it was false that p as while it was true that p. (We might think of such deliverances as ostensible indications, as when it is ostensibly perceived that p—ostensibly seen, or heard, etc.—or, perhaps, ostensibly intuited, and so on.)[17]

Next let us consider "obstacles" to veridical perception. What is an obstacle and what makes it so? Here are some potential instances:

DD. Defective perceptual dispositions [exercised in believing that p]

MC. Misleading perceptual conditions [involved in one's manifesting those dispositions through one's belief that p]

After all, this last says no more than:

4. My belief Bp has source X and it is true that p.

And 4 is just a matter of conjoining 1 and 2. So, given knowledge of 1 and 2, one can trivially conclude that one's source is "veridical" in yielding one's belief Bp.

[17] This idea is developed some in my "Tracking, Competence, and Knowledge," in Paul Moser (ed.), *The Oxford Handbook of Epistemology* (Oxford: OUP, 2002), pp. 264–87.

Presumably these are obstacles to *veridical* perception because they somehow obstruct our access to the truth of the target belief through our exercise of the relevant perceptual dispositions in favorable conditions. We are in effect said to need evidence that, in coming to believe that p, the dispositions we exercise are not relevantly deficient and the conditions involved in their exercise are not relevantly misleading. Not too easily can those dispositions deliver falsehood when exercised in those conditions.[18]

If we must rule out the likes of DD and MC before we can have perceptual knowledge (or even coordinately with

[18] Compare the obstacles in the text with the following:

DD' Defective perceptual dispositions that in fact deliver a falsehood [in giving one to believe that p]

DD" Misleading perceptual conditions involved in the exercise of our relevant perceptual dispositions that deliver a falsehood [simply as a matter of fact, in giving one to believe that p]

When we enjoy perceptual knowledge based on how things look to us, we are said to need more than just the look of things. We need also to know, at least to presuppose, or take it for granted, that epistemic obstacles are absent. What is the nature of these obstacles? Are they the likes of DD and MC, or are they rather like the primed correlates, DD' and MC'?

If the obstacles are only the primed correlates, then we can see how to rule them out through our knowledge that p. Indeed, given knowledge of 1 (i.e., <p>) and 2 (i.e., <My belief Bp has source X>), above, this can of course yield knowledge of 4 (i.e., <My belief Bp has source X and it is true that p>), as we have seen. And this is tantamount to ruling out these primed obstacles, so long as perceptually knowing that p would be tantamount to getting it right in believing that p, thus manifesting certain perceptual dispositions (epistemic abilities or competences) in certain perceptual conditions, all of which would amount to the belief's having the source X involved in 4.

SUPPOSE that we must rule out *with priority* the relevant epistemic obstacles on the way to perceptual knowledge that p (or must at least do so *without posteriority*). IF SO, the obstacles would then seem to be *not* the primed obstacles but their correlates: DD and MC. For one thing, knowledge of 4 (i.e., <My belief Bp has source X and it is true that p>), or equivalently of 3 (i.e., <In yielding my belief Bp, source X is veridical, just as a matter of fact >), could hardly be *prior* to knowledge that p. (Here I assume that knowledge of a conjunction would be based on knowledge of the conjuncts distributively, and not conversely.)

having it), however, how then could we first acquire such knowledge? How could we come to know, about certain of our perceptual dispositions, that they are not deficient (that on the contrary they constitute abilities, capacities, competences), and, about certain perceptual conditions in which those dispositions are exercised, that these are not misleading?[19]

This problem must be faced if we insist that perceptual knowledge requires knowledge that one's sources are reliable, even if the knowledge is implicit.[20] How then do we gain this knowledge? Does the solution to the problem of easy knowledge require that we allow such knowledge of our own reliability, and if so how can we possibly acquire it?[21]

IV. How to Turn the Problem of Easy Knowledge into a Proof of Skepticism

Given the way "basic" knowledge is understood, there is bound to be basic knowledge that is sophisticated and not just animal, so long as there is sophisticated non-animal knowledge at all.[22] To see this more clearly, we must distinguish two sorts of basicness:

---

[19] What sort of deficiency is involved? In what relevant way might we be misled? These are of course epistemic matters: the deficiency or the misleading character is presumably that of putting us insufficiently in touch with the truth.

[20] Relevant here is our discussion in section I of what is involved in source reliability.

[21] And the problem remains even if the "implicit knowledge" here is a kind of quasi-knowledge, or even just a matter of being in a position to know. We will still require an explanation of what induces such quasi-knowledge, or what puts one in such a position, and the dialectic of circularity will still be triggered thereby.

[22] This is compatible with the fact that there could not possibly be any basic *reflective* knowledge, since this latter sort of knowledge is *defined* so as to preclude that possibility.

Kp is inferentially basic iff it is not based on inference, so its sources are not inferential.

Kp is hierarchically basic iff it is held unaccompanied by knowledge that its basis (or, more generally, its source) is reliable.

Thus, a bit of knowledge could be inferentially basic without being hierarchically basic, and a bit of knowledge could be hierarchically basic without being inferentially basic.

Now, an epistemology is said to count as BKS (as having a Basic Knowledge Structure) iff it commits to the following two theses:

T1.   There is hierarchically basic knowledge.
T2.   Such basic knowledge gives a basis for knowing that the sources of one's knowledge are reliable [that one's embedded belief is based reliably, both specifically and generically].

What are we to think of BKS epistemologies?

Every plausible epistemology will satisfy the first requirement for being a BKS epistemology, since it is impossible for humans *actually* to ascend infinite ladders of reflection. Reflection is bound to give out at some level, where we no longer have an explicit or implicit belief of the form $B^{n+1}p$ although we do have a belief of the form $B^n p$ (where the superscripts represent the number of levels involved).

A proof for skepticism sets out from that fact as its first premise:

(a)   If there is human knowledge at all, then there is hierarchically basic human knowledge.
(b)   If one knows that p in a hierarchically basic way then one can come to know, based partly on this

knowledge, that the basis for this knowledge (or its embedded belief) is specifically or generically reliable.

(c) In no case where one knows that p can one come to know, based even just partly on this knowledge, that the basis for this knowledge (or its embedded belief) is specifically or generically reliable.

(d) Therefore, there is no human knowledge.

For most of us this proof is a reductio. If obviously there is some human knowledge, then, given that premise (a) is indisputable, we can conclude instead that either (b) or (c) must be false.

Again, if obviously there *is* hierarchically basic knowledge (which entails premise (a), materially understood), then T1 is uncontroversial and the focus is on the second commitment of a BKS epistemology (tantamount to premise b), as follows:

T2. One's basic knowledge gives one a basis for knowing that the basis of that knowledge is reliable [that the basis for one's embedded belief is reliable].

This is in line with the following two possibilities:

T2′ One's hierarchically basic knowledge that p gives a basis (at least a partial basis, even if not a conclusive, deductive basis) for one to know that one's basis for then knowing that p is a *specifically* reliable basis.

T2″ One's hierarchically basic knowledge that p gives a basis (at least a partial basis) for one to know that one's basis for then knowing that p is a *generically* reliable basis.

And one might of course *combine* T2′ and T2″ for a two-fold conjunctive principle.

T2′ corresponds to the reasoning from one's belief that the wall one sees is red, based on the look of the wall taken at face value, to the conclusion that the wall is not white bathed in misleading light. By contrast, T2″ corresponds to simple inductive bootstrapping from the repeated success of source X to the conclusion that source X is reliable, where the database for one's inductive inference derives only from one's repeatedly trusting source X despite not then knowing it to be reliable.

Is this the way beyond our reductio? Should we reject thesis T2 (premise b)?[23] Is this our best way out?

---

[23] Thesis T2 endorses the inference to the propitiousness of one's situation, and also the simple inductive bootstrapping to the generic reliability of one's source. But neither of these seems acceptable. Why is that?

Some argue that the appearance here is just misleading, that the inference is acceptable as a way to know its conclusion, although it corresponds to an argument that would be question-begging if addressed to someone else who had put in question the propitiousness of one's situation or the generic reliability of one's source. "Although the reasoning involved would be thus *dialectically* defective" we are told, "if offered against any such skeptic, it is still perfectly *epistemically* in order as provider of epistemic status for its conclusion. One *can* in fact come to know about the propitiousness of one's situation by inference from one's basic knowledge, and one *can* in fact come to know about the generic reliability of one's source by simple bootstrapping from a database acquired only by repeatedly trusting that source despite *not* at those times knowing it to be generically reliable."

Helpful though it is to distinguish thus between the use of an argument as a tool of rational persuasion and its use as a means or source of discovery, this seems implausible as a solution for the problem of easy knowledge. For, when wholly ignorant of the propitiousness of one's circumstances, and wholly ignorant of the generic reliability of one's source, one could hardly *discover* that one's source is specifically or generically reliable by *concluding* this from one's basic knowledge deriving *only* from the use of that source in those circumstances, nor even by concluding it from one's *having* such basic knowledge. Compare section II above. One could hardly gain all epistemic status for one's relevant presuppositions about one's epistemic situation through inference from the knowledge that one enjoys only with the benefit of such presuppositions. So the question will remain as to how such presuppositions can gain the required epistemic status. (I am here skirting the distinction between each of DD and MC and its primed correlate,

V. The Importance of Commitments

Distinguish first implicit from consciously explicit *belief*; and, correspondingly, implicit from consciously explicit *knowledge*. Consider next a subject S who believes at t that the wall before him is red, <Rw>, while taking its look at face value. I might implicitly discern that my situation is propitious for taking such experience at face value, without being explicitly conscious of that fact. I might even raise my consciousness of it, moreover, through explicit reasoning that involves <Rw>. What remains implausible is that I should attain epistemic justification for my then presupposing that my situation is propitious for taking my color experience thus at face value, and that I should *first* attain such justification even partly through reasoning (implicit or explicit) that requires my *prior* knowledge that I see a red wall.

However, one need not even insist on the *words* here. Advert rather to the fact that there are *commitments* (let's call them that), implicit states of the subject who "takes for granted" or "presupposes" that his situation is propitious (and his source generically reliable). Such commitments have the following profile. They are

- *contingent* states, ones that subjects can be in or fail to be in;
- states with propositional content; and
- states epistemically evaluable in the sorts of ways in which beliefs tend to be epistemically evaluable.

Given this profile, the basic point can still be made, even without insisting that these implicit commitments constitute

DD' or MC'. Correspondingly, I am also ignoring the status of ascent from Kp to KKp, at least upon consideration of Kp. I myself believe that such ascent is defensible.)

"knowledge" strictly so-called. We might speak of "quasi-knowledge" if it seems important to distinguish commitments from beliefs. For, the basic point is this: It is most implausible that from one's belief that one sees a red wall, or even from one's belief that one thereby acquires perceptual knowledge, one can *gain* proper epistemic status for one's implicit commitments about how specifically or generically reliable one's basis then is for so believing. One could hardly start with no proper status for these commitments and then acquire the belief that one sees a red wall or even that one knows oneself to see a red wall, and then, *posterior to that*, acquire proper epistemic status for one's relevant commitments. *Note that this does not rule out one's acquiring epistemic status in one package deal*, both for the belief that one sees a red wall, and conjointly for the relevant commitments, and that the epistemic status of the commitments depends in part (perhaps in small part) on the fact that they are now based in part (perhaps in small part) on one's belief that one sees a red wall. That seems to me far from implausible, and may well be true. (We return to this idea in due course.)

What does remain implausible nonetheless, and to involve a kind of vicious circle, is the following:

(a) that one should be entirely lacking in epistemic status for the relevant implicit commitments about the propitiousness of one's situation (and the generic reliability of one's source) in believing that one sees a red wall (that these commitments should be entirely *unjustified* epistemically),

(b) that one should then become justified epistemically in believing that one does see a red wall (acquire epistemic status for that belief) without yet being at all justified in one's commitments (without having proper epistemic status for hosting those commitments),

and

(c) that *then*, based on one's belief about the wall's color, and on one's already acquired justification for that belief, one should *thereby* acquire relevant justification (epistemic status) for hosting those commitments.

If the proposition *that he sees a red wall* is believed by someone *based* on his color experience,[24] moreover, this belief then presumably manifests an implicit commitment to some generalization of the form: <when things look this way, I am seeing a red wall>, or perhaps of the form: <when things look this way, I am seeing something red>. So, the implicit commitment may then *be present* and *operative* when one forms such a belief on such a basis.

That leaves it open what form the "commitment" might take. It might take the form of an explicit belief, but it might rather be an implicit belief, or even just a forbearing from blocking the normal operation of a perceptual module. In any case it will be some state or doing of one's own, one possessed of propositional content, and one assessable epistemically as proper or not, justified or not, competent or not, or some such. Beliefs can be well formed or not, and based on reasons, despite being largely involuntary and implicit. It is hard to see why presuppositional commitments could not share such normative features.

Accordingly, what we are supposing in (a) must be that one does not at that point yet have any epistemic justification (epistemic status) for sustaining that commitment. So, one at

---

[24] Plus other psychological states of one's own concerning the situation one takes oneself to be in, but I will ignore these for simplicity in what follows.

that point forms the belief that one sees a red wall, manifesting in so doing an *unjustified* commitment (*epistemically*
unjustified, i.e., lacking in proper epistemic status). One then
supposedly acquires thereby an epistemically justified belief
that one sees a red wall. And only then is one able to reach
some epistemically appropriate affirmative attitude, implicit
or explicit, about the content of that theretofore unjustified
commitment.

It seems out of the question that epistemic justification
could be generated *ex nihilo* that way. The problem resides
in the ex nihilo generation of normative status and not in the
nature of the bearer of that status, which on any account is
some contingent state or event in which the subject figures,
and one whose normative status requires an explanatory
source. The normative status of the subject's belief that
he sees a red wall cannot derive from the presence and
operation of that commitment (whatever its nature) while the
commitment acquires *its* normative status only *posteriorly* to
the belief's having its proper status. How could the belief have
its proper epistemic status through an *unjustified* (*a not justified*)
commitment, one without proper epistemic status of its own?

Our discussion has been restricted, as predicted near the
outset, to epistemic sources or faculties that are reason-based,
whereby beliefs are formed or sustained on the basis of reasons
operative at the time when the belief is present. Thus, our
discussion may be fine as far as it goes, while falling short that
way. We are thus led to the Problem of the Criterion.

VI. Easy Knowledge and the Criterion

Suppose one is disposed to acquire and sustain beliefs in a certain way, and suppose one wonders whether this disposition

reliably yields beliefs that are true. It would seem viciously circular to answer that it is indeed reliable, whether in the specific instance or generically, based just on deliverances of that very disposition. Why so? Is it because such a disposition must operate with the aid of presuppositions that in effect already amount to the claim that it is indeed reliable? If so, then of course one could hardly *discover* that it is reliable through its own operation, since its operation requires a prior or correlative commitment to its own reliability. Yet it is far from obvious, and seems in fact false, that our epistemic competences generally operate through such presuppositions, through presuppositions, for example, like those one might find in our perceptual competences.

Epistemic competences that are *not* reason-based do not plausibly involve such presuppositions, however plausibly these may be involved in those that *are* reason based.[25] So, no general solution to the problem of easy knowledge can be restricted to reason-based competences, and that includes our earlier proposed solution, which is perforce only partial. The solution to the general problem cannot require that the operation of a competence will always involve a presupposition that we must implicitly know or quasi-know, whose epistemic status cannot possibly derive wholly from the epistemic status of the deliverances of that competence, since these deliverances owe their status essentially to the presupposition's already or coordinately having that status.

---

[25] Reason-based competences are those that properly weigh reasons in the fixing of belief. Beliefs not based on reasons can also be "competently" held, in assuming which I may be stretching the term. In any case, they can be "properly" held. (As for the "weighing" of reasons, this need not be conscious or deliberate, which may again involve a stretch. By such weighing I mean just the reason's exerting a certain amount of influence on how one believes on the matter at hand, and this need not be something one guides deliberately or even consciously.)

It is not only presuppositions, with their propositional content, that need epistemically normative status, however, if they are properly to help constitute a (reason-based) competence. In fact, epistemic competences generally, whether reason-based or not, require proper epistemic status if they are to deliver the epistemic goods. Of course, when we think of a disposition as a "competence" we already assign to it a normatively positive status. Something must explain a disposition's having that status, however, and for epistemic dispositions the relevant consideration would seem to be importantly truth-reliability. (Even the Internalist Foundationalist-in-Chief of the tradition considered such reliability a *sine qua non*.)

Nevertheless, not every problem of easy knowledge that affects reason-based competences need similarly affect competences generally, including those that, since not reason-based, seem therefore free of the constitutive presuppositions that can plausibly be found in the special case of perception (and perhaps in reason-based competences generally). After all, if a competence might even do its work sub-personally, it is wildly implausible that the subject of that competence should be blocked (by some worry about vicious circularity) from discovering the specifics and even the reliability of the sub-personal mechanisms involved, from discovering this indeed through the deliverances of that very competence.[26] Thus

---

[26] Here one might naturally be led to wonder: "How can it be such a problem earlier on if it is wildly implausible that there is a problem here? In other words, how does the problem even get off the ground in the preceding chapter if it is wildly implausible that there is a circularity problem here?" The reason is that with reason-based faculties, or at least with perception in particular, implicit presuppositions are in play (or so I have argued) that cannot derive their status wholly from the deliverances whose own status *presupposes* (and thus cannot endow) the status of the implicit presuppositions. Moreover, the implicit presuppositions, the "commitments," seem to be empirical and not the sort of thing that could have a priori foundational status.

compare the discovery of how our vision works reliably and what makes it reliable, a discovery based essentially (not just causally but normatively) on the visual observations of scientists.[27]

Competence that is not reason-based, whose reliable modus-operandi may be essentially sub-personal, depends for its epistemic standing on no justificatory performance by its owner. Such animal competence comes fundamentally with our endowment at birth or is triggered sub-personally through normal early development. What gives it *epistemic* standing, moreover, is in essential part its animal reliability in enabling the harvest of needful information.

While especially plausible for competences that are *not* reason-based, that account is not much less plausible for reason-based competences as well, such as, on our account, perception in its many guises. This just means that the epistemic standing of taking experience at face value, absent special reason for suspicion, derives from its serving

---

[27] "But vision is a form of perception. So how could there be a problem of easy knowledge involving perception but not vision?" The *fuller* faculty of vision would provide an explanation of what makes it the case that our implicit commitment repeatedly to take visual experience at face value is as reliable as it is. Our specific implicit commitments, in situation after situation that we enter with open eyes, to take our visual experiences again at face value, are themselves delivered by a competence, one that is itself constitutive of the faculty of vision (i.e., the *commitments* themselves are so delivered). *This* competence (to deliver such commitments in situation after situation) is itself a reliable disposition. This disposition is not reason-based, however. It is rather part of our animal endowment. But there is presumably an explanation, one involving rods and cones, the optic nerve, etc., as to why it is that this disposition is itself a competence. And this explanation, finally, can be arrived at by vision scientists at least in part through the exercise of the very competence whose reliability is being explained. What seems quite implausible is that these scientists should be precluded by some worry about *circularity* from discovering the reliability of such non-reason-based dispositions.

us reliably well in the harvest of information proper to a well-functioning human organism.

Our trust in our animal epistemic competences is thus a source of epistemic standing for the beliefs thus acquired simply because those competences themselves, those animal faculties, have a proper epistemic standing of their own, which they derive from being part of the animal endowment of an epistemically well-functioning human being.[28]

VII. Rational Justification: the Reflective and the Unreflective

It would be quite wrong, however, to conclude that epistemic justification could not be generated through any "circular" procedure. In order to see the potential, we need to distinguish between unreflective (animal) justification and reflective justification. And let us now restrict ourselves to unreflective *rational* justification and reflective *rational* justification.

Unreflective justification, animal justification, depends on no reflective endorsement: on no endorsement of the *specific reliability* of one's basis (or at least of the *safety* of that basis, of the fact that it would not lead one astray in delivering the deliverance that p). *Nor* does such rational justification depend on any endorsement of the *generic reliability* of one's basis. It can nevertheless be rational justification in deriving from the believer's basing of his belief on a reason that he has

---

[28] That epistemology is hence close kin to the kind distinguished by Stewart Cohen as BKS ("basic knowledge structure"), for it recognizes a crucial sort of epistemic standing, animal competence, which is attained without the aid of any metabelief that endorses any such competence as reliable.

and thus uses. So it is for basic reason-based competences, such as much of our perceptual endowment.

Reflective rational justification, by contrast, is acquired at least in part through rational endorsement: *either* through endorsement of the *specific reliability* of one's basis (or at least of the *safety* of one's basis, of the fact that it would not lead one astray in delivering the deliverance that p), *or* through endorsement of the *generic reliability* of one's basis.

We have seen how implausible it is that unreflective justification for one's explicit or implicit commitments should be generated entirely through reasoning based on beliefs acquired only through *unjustified* (or *epistemically inappropriate*) commitments. Consider, on the other hand, one's justification for a given commitment (or its status as epistemically appropriate): say a commitment that lies behind one's belief that one sees a red wall. Might one's *reflective* rational justification for that commitment gain a boost through one's now basing it in part (perhaps in some very small part) on the belief that one does see a red wall. How are we to understand such a boost in reflective rational justification?

VIII. Epistemic Justification: Pipeline versus Web

The right model for understanding reflective justification is *not* the linear model whereby justification is a sort of liquid that flows through some pipe or channel of reasoning, from premises to conclusion. (Such flow is linear, unidirectional; the pipe or channel "transmits" the justification—or warrant, or epistemic status.) A better model is rather that of the web of belief, whereby the web is properly attached to the environment, while its nodes can also gain status through mutual support. Any given node is thus in place through its connections with other nodes, but *each of them* is itself in place through *its* connections with the other nodes, including that original given node. By basing beliefs on other beliefs the rational weaver weaves a web each member of which is held in place *in part* (perhaps in minuscule part) through its being based on certain others, directly or indirectly. There is no apparent reason why such basing should be regarded as either causally or normatively asymmetrical, no reason why many beliefs could not constitute webs in which *each* node is in place by being based *partly* on the *others*. What is more, each might thus gain its epistemic status partly through such relations with the others, where the whole web is also attached to the world through the causal mechanisms of perception and memory.

Reflective endorsement may now take its place in the web without any apparent special problems. Through our growing commonsense and scientific knowledge of ourselves and of the world around us and of the relation between the two, we see our modes of rational basing and other belief acquisition as sufficiently reliable. This enables us to endorse such modes reflectively as truth-reliable and hence of a sort to lend *epistemic* justification to our commitments and beliefs. Of course, when in psychology or neurobiology or cognitive science or common sense we modify an epistemic commitment, whether implicit or explicit, we do so based on beliefs that we acquire through our relevant commitments already in place, prominently those involved in our perceptual acquisition of information. There is hence an inevitable circle involved in the way we come to modify and hold our relevant perceptual commitments, whether implicit or explicit. For we hold them, and sustain them over time, based on continuing observations, and on particular perceptual beliefs, which are themselves based on the now installed, and perhaps modified commitments. There seems no special viciousness pertaining to the nodes of our web constituted by these commitments.

Suppose, for example, that my web contains a commitment that underlies my reacting to visual experience as of a red wall by believing that I see something red. This commitment would seem to have some propositional content such as the following:

If I have a visual experience as of seeing something red, then I see something red,

which ostensibly amounts to a reliability claim as follows:

Reliably, if I have a visual experience as of seeing something red, I tend to see something red.[29]

This can figure in the acquisition by a scientific observer of a perceptual belief that she sees something red. And what can possibly preclude such a scientific datum from helping to confirm some generalization in the psychology of perception, one that might eventually bear, however minimally, on our justification for taking human color vision to be truth-reliable, and also on our justification for trusting our own color vision?

---

[29] The content of this "commitment" is not easy to discern. It does not seem to be a perfectly general proposition of the form "Whenever I seem to see something red, I do see something red." Nor does it seem a general statistical claim. What one brings to any given situation with open eyes is a commitment to the proposition that if one *then* has an appearance as of seeing something red, one does *then* see something red. And so on. Might one not be so constituted that one would bring such a commitment to any arbitrary situation, without being committed to any purely general closed proposition to the effect that always, or even generally, one's perceptual appearances (of red) are veridical? Perhaps one needs at least a commitment to a properly qualified "tendency" or 'habitual" proposition.

But how can it be acceptable to use perceptual knowledge as a basis, however partial, for the epistemic status of the implicit or explicit commitments that underwrite our retail perceptual knowledge, as in the scientific observations whereby we acquire our empirical data? How can that be acceptable, if it is acceptable *neither* to indulge in *simple* bootstrapping *nor* to reason from our perceptual belief directly to the conclusion that we are well situated for such perception? Answer: It must be recognized that, by parity of reasoning, the mutual support even in these latter cases might add *something* of epistemic value. Coherence through mutual support seems a matter of degree, and even the minimal degree involved in simple bootstrapping is not worthless. Nor does it seem worthless even when it turns out that both the particular perceptual belief *and* the commitment are false. Mutually supportive comprehensive coherence is always worth something, even if its value is vanishingly small when it remains this simple, especially when the web is detached from the surrounding world because it is false through and through. This is all compatible with the enhancements that derive from increasing richness and from increasing attachments to the world beyond. Suppose we steadily enrich our comprehensive coherence, with more reliable, truth-involving connections with our world. This might come about either via our cognitive community, or individually on our own, or both.

Presumably, with such gains would come enhanced understanding.[30] Why suppose that no gain can possibly accrue to an individual perceptual belief based on an epistemic

[30] A full account of epistemically acceptable comprehensive coherence would include ways to deal with Goodman's gruesome possibilities, with Hempel's ravens paradox, and with excessive epicyclic complexity.

perspective constituted by such implicit commitments, and now also by the subject's more explicit understanding of his epistemic situation and ways of knowing? It seems incredible that we could not *somehow* use our faculties to gain access to knowledge of our own reliability, to knowledge of the ways in which, and the extent to which we are reliable, at least in rough outline.[31]

We are soon disposed to form beliefs of certain sorts perceptually and to store those that we may need in due course. These dispositions, perhaps innate, perhaps triggered subpersonally through normal infancy, receive little or no benefit of *rational* development or support, at least in any early stages of their tenure. That of course changes dramatically in later stages, as we become more rationally complete beings in fuller rational control.

---

[31] Reflective knowledge helps to guide its corresponding animal belief. Proper reflective knowledge must after all satisfy requirements of coherence, which means not just logical or probabilistic coherence of the respective belief contents, but also the mutual basing relations that can properly reflect such coherence among the contents. Cross-level coherence, from the object to the meta, and conversely, is a special case of such coherence. And with *such* coherence comes "guidance" of the animal belief by the relevant meta-beliefs (or, in other words, basing of the former on the latter). It bears emphasis that the meta-aptness of a belief, which I argue in forthcoming work to be an important factor in its *epistemic* evaluation, requires ascent to a good enough perspective on the first-level potential attitudes among which the subject must opt (whether he opts with full conscious deliberation or through a less explicit procedure). Coherence among first-level attitudes is not enough. The subject must ascend to a level wherein he performs cost/benefit analysis, whether in full consciousness or less explicitly, and eventually opts on that basis. In order to yield a fully creditable performance, finally, such analysis must take into account one's relevant competence(s) and situation, and must do so with epistemic appropriateness.

Index